The Wrecking Storm

The second Thomas Tallant Adventure

MICHAEL WARD

For Jamie, Rachel and Sophie

CONTENTS

Prologue

The River Thames
May 9th 1641

A chill wind blew upriver as the dawn struggled into life. London was waking to a dank, grey day, the overnight rain still pulsing fitfully, peppering the water's surface.

A wherry edged from its landing stage on the northern bank of the Thames. As the boat cleared the dock, small waves slapped against its side, making the lantern in its prow bob up and down, a solitary movement on the black, silent expanse of water.

Francis Cavendish shuddered and gathered his thin cloak around his shoulders.

Sitting at the back of the wherry, he was chilled to the marrow, but didn't care. He had finally escaped from the suffocating hole in the wall that had been his hiding place for three weeks.

He studied the broad-shouldered man on his right sharing his seat. Francis did not know his name, where he came from or who he was. And yet he was trusting this swarthy stranger with his life.

Instead of fear, he experienced an intense elation. Two days ago he was within inches of discovery, certain torture and a bloody death, only to escape! In that moment, he knew the Lord still had work for him.

His throat tightened and nausea returned at the memory of that priest hole – the shouts on the stairwell, the tramp of boots and then hammering on the wall outside his hiding place. Voices yelling, wood splintering, excited shouts of discovery turning to curses and oaths, and then silence. Francis, a cloth rammed into his mouth to stifle the sobs of panic convulsing his body, straining his every fibre to be still, and all the time the murmur of voices inches from him, disappointed, bitter. And, finally, the desultory clatter as his armed pursuers walked away, disappointed. He had escaped discovery by the thickness of an oak panel. His 'hide within a hide' had deceived his pursuers as intended. It was a miracle.

Francis was transferred that night to an old warehouse by the river, and there he remained until his rescuers arrived in the early hours of this morning. Now he was afloat, heading to safety.

A ragged cormorant emerged from the gloom and scudded past the wherry in full flight, only feet above the water's surface. The man on his right yawned and coughed. Silence had been critical when they left the warehouse but now they were approaching mid-river. The man stretched and nodded towards the priest's head, looking quizzically. 'Why have you kept it?'

Francis touched his shock of red hair and grimaced. 'I usually dye it black but I had to leave my last refuge in something of a hurry.'

'Mmm, that's a pity. You don't want to stand out and be remembered.'

Francis nodded. He studied the man's face in the improving light. His leathery skin was ravaged by smallpox scars, his lank, straw-coloured hair tucked behind his ears, revealing piercing blue eyes.

The stranger had arrived at the old warehouse with two others. Francis had been wary but, despite his fierce appearance, the man was calm and respectful. He provided much needed food and drink and joined him in prayers before eating. Francis noted the stranger's care in avoiding discovery as they left the warehouse, and his conviction grew that he was in safe hands.

But why was their progress now so slow? Francis longed to be away from London and, as the gloom lifted, he could see the other two men in the wherry more clearly. Only one was rowing, while the other sat in the prow holding the lantern.

The man next to him rummaged in his cloak and pulled out a leather flask, which he opened and offered with a smile. 'Here, brother. Take a drink of this. It'll give you warmth as the Lord gives you strength. Now we're away from the shore, we can talk more freely. My name is Dancer, Jack Dancer, and it's my honour to provide safe passage for yourself, a member of the blessed Society of Jesus, away from this benighted and godless country. Our plan is to row downriver to Gravesend where we'll meet up with a sailing barque bound for France when the tide and winds are right.'

Francis coughed as he swallowed the rough brandy, then savoured its warmth spreading across his chest from his throat. 'Thank you, Jack,' Francis said, returning the flask. 'God bless you for arranging my escape. I have recently seen the Lord still has important work for me.'

'Amen to that,' Jack replied, crossing himself. 'The work of the Jesuit brotherhood is a wonder and solace to all of us who follow the true faith. It must make great demands and take you to many different parts of the world.' Francis smiled. Once they knew he was a Jesuit, fellow Catholics would always press him, eyes alight, for accounts of his missions to foreign lands and success in converting lost souls. It was the first thing they wanted to hear and it appeared that this man Jack, even in their current parlous situation, was no different.

So, as the oars creaked and they inched their way down river, Francis recounted his last mission in New France in North America, converting Algonquin natives. After three years, he returned to Paris with a burning wish to spread the Catholic faith still further in the New World.

But he was forced to grapple with the sin of personal

disappointment when, instead of a return to North America, he was sent to England. Mass must be held by a priest but to do so publicly in England now invited discovery and punishment by the authorities. He was one of several Jesuits spirited into the country to provide secret support. However, he had not expected his movements to be so restricted, and now felt unfulfilled.

He spent much of his time in hiding, moved from house to house by his persecuted hosts. He despaired of ever doing God's work again and then, last week, the Lord had saved him from the jaws of his enemy. He was still part of God's plan. Suffused with the inner glow of his rediscovered conviction, Francis's heart filled with joy. Had Jesus saved him for this? A return to the Algonquin?

Jack listened intently, not asking questions. Eventually he turned to Francis. 'That is most interesting and uplifting brother. And did your missionary work take you elsewhere, say, eastwards towards the Indies and the Orient?'

'No, not all, my future lies with the Algonquin, I am sure. But I believe we have other brothers doing God's work in Goa, and Macau.' The conversation petered out and soon Francis became increasingly aware of the cold and his aching bones. He prayed he was not coming down with ague.

Jack moved away and carefully stood to view the way ahead. Gripping Francis's shoulder to help him balance, he leaned forward and spoke quietly into the ear of the man rowing the wherry. The man nodded and Jack returned to the stern seat, next to Francis.

'Are we making good progress?' Francis asked. 'I fear my aching joints tell me I'm becoming too old for these adventures.'

Dancer twisted in his seat to face Francis. 'Yes, almost journey's end.'

Francis experienced a painful punch in his lower chest and looked down, bemused, at his shirt and leggings, now soaking in his own, warm blood. Jack gripped his shoulder, pulling him closer while he pushed the knife in, up to its hilt. He gazed into the priest's eyes, which were staring back, wild with shock.

'As I said Francis, I am honoured to be your fellow traveller on your final journey. Hold me tight, brother. I am the means of your deliverance.'

In the midst of his disbelief, Francis frantically sought certainty. I am called to Jesu? Why now? But there was no time left for answers. His inner body was collapsing, his mind not far behind. His senses were draining away, all conscious awareness narrowing to a pinhole of light in the enveloping darkness, and a final, echoing word: 'why?'

Dancer gently removed the long blade from the Jesuit's chest and placed it carefully on the floor of the wherry. Still holding him close, he pulled back his hood, stroked strands of ginger hair from his victim's face and kissed his forehead.

'It is a mercy I have delivered, Francis. You had no future, hunted to extinction like a rat. Now you have died in the glory of presumption, believing you have been called.'

Dancer's companion manning the oars had paused to witness the murder. The young man laughed and sneered: 'Sacrifice? They're all beggin' for it, you know that Jack. You do 'em a service.'

Jack Dancer put his finger to his lips to silence the man, shaking his head gently in admonishment. 'That's enough of that, Billy Boy. Have some respect. Now hand me the necessary.' The young man passed a heavy sack to Dancer, who chose several large rocks from within and filled the priest's cloak pockets, before effortlessly lifting his corpse and slipping it silently into the Thames.

Within seconds, the mortal remains of Francis Cavendish slid beneath the surface of the Thames and disappeared, without a bubble or a ripple.

Chapter 1

The Tallant warehouse

Thomas Tallant leaned back in his chair and studied the woman sitting in front of him. 'So, you are, or rather were, married to Josh Wilding?'

The woman's face was buried in a rag, which muffled her weeping. She nodded her head vigorously between sobs, but her makeshift handkerchief stayed in place. Tom looked past the woman and through the open loading bay, to the Thames beyond. The grey cloud had lifted, revealing a clear blue sky which silhouetted her hunched figure. Lord, he'd rather be on the river this fine spring day.

He returned to his visitor. 'In that case, I'm sure you can give me a description of his features?'

Once more she dissolved into a bout of sobbing but moved the rag sufficiently to mumble a few words: 'I be too upset to talk about it'.

At this point, the tall distinguished figure of his father Sir Ralph Tallant, entered the room. He nodded at Tom and went to stand at the back, his arms folded.

Josh Wilding had crewed on their recent sailing to Amsterdam, a short voyage but on the way home he'd slipped off the rigging in heavy seas and hit the deck hard. News of his demise came with the ship's return to dock three days ago.

'Well perhaps you could tell me his hair colour. Could you manage that?'

There was a long pause. Then a mumbled reply. 'He be fair, well fair-ish. Maybe closer to brown.'

Tom sighed and stood up. 'Enough. This show is over.' This

7

produced further muted protests from the woman. He lost his patience and pulled the cloth out of her grasp, to reveal an angry, dry-eyed face.

'What d'you think you're about, treating a poor widow like this,' the woman shouted. 'All I want is his wages from his last trip. That's mine by rights and you know it! Shame on you, with all your money, trying to cheat a poor widow, and with four hungry children to feed. The money's mine, and I have the proof!' and she pointed at the table in front of her.

Tom picked up a dirty, creased scrap of paper. A last will and testament in the name of Josh Wilding, in a handwritten scrawl, leaving all his worldly goods to his wife Anne.

'There it be, in black and white. Everything left to Anne. That's me, that is.' And she pushed her chin out in indignation.

At least she's trying, Tom thought. More than the others. 'Well Anne, if that's your name, Josh Wilding's hair was as black as coal. He used to say it came from the Irish side of his family. That's something we'd expect his wife to know, isn't it?'

Anne sat in her chair and gave him a murderous look. He frowned. This was becoming increasingly common, and tiresome. When a ship docked, news of a death on board spread quickly. Thieves would use any means to discover the name in question, and the next day they'd be at the warehouse door, will and testament in hand, the ink barely dry.

Before they sailed, some crew informed owners exactly who to pay if they didn't return. Wilding was a lively, carefree character. A bit of a rascal but likeable enough. Not the will-writing kind, of that Tom was sure. So he felt a duty to ensure the true next of kin received their due.

'Right, you've wasted enough of my time.' He shouted to the next room. 'Isaac, escort this woman from the building.' His warehouse manager emerged from the parlour to take the woman's arm.

'Don't touch me,' she snarled and leapt up, jabbing her finger at Tom.

'Think you're so high and mighty don't you, mister. Sitting here, surrounded by all your money. What difference would it make to give me a shilling or two? God knows I need it. So, you caught me out. Very clever. But mark my words. Times are changing for me and my type, and we'll be back to get our fair share of the money swimming around your warehouse, and this city. And next time, we won't come cap in hand!'

'Right, call the constable,' Tom ordered, but the woman was already striding from the room, leaving her 'proof' on the table. He shook his head. 'Do we know if Wilding had family?'

'No,' Isaac replied. 'We got him from the press. Sailed ordinary with us a couple of times and gave a decent account of himself. I'll ask around in the Swan and see if I can track his kin.'

Tom stood and walked to the parlour fire, warming his hands on the sea coal burning red hot in the grate. His father joined him.

'We've had two previous claims this week for the wages of young Wilding,' Ralph confided. 'Yesterday, it was someone professing to be his destitute old father. He stank of ale and could not even get his son's name right under my questioning.'

'But why do they do it? They must know we will check?'

Ralph took a mug of ale offered by Isaac and eased his six foot frame into the seat vacated by the woman. 'Not all owners do, so they think it's worth a try. Many are desperate. Tempted to London by tales of easy money, they find there's nowhere to live, food they can't afford and pestilence everywhere. But did you notice her sense of entitlement, of grievance? - 'we'll be back to get our *fair share*?... *Times are changing*.' The people are getting bold, Tom, starting to revolt. I'm told there were thousands this morning, swarming like flies around the gates of the Royal Palace, calling for the head of the Earl of Strafford. They're over-stepping the mark. Retribution will follow, you can be sure'.

'I see John Pym's work here,' Ralph continued, 'and the Puritan MPs he leads against the King. He's like a puppet master, with Parliament in one hand and the mob and their rumours in the other, working them in harness to pressure the King. But Pym's picked the wrong fight this time, trying to bring down Strafford, and it's been over six months since he was impeached. He's the King's right hand man and Charles has promised the Earl he will be safe. The King can't afford to lose him, or his authority.'

'Anyway, let us turn our mind to more pleasant matters. I had the most stimulating discussion with young Elizabeth Seymour yesterday that has left my mind quite spinning.'

Tom knew the feeling only too well. He had met Elizabeth on his return from India nineteen months ago. He had been completely smitten and now they were rarely apart.

'Yes, she was talking to me about the moons of Jupiter and how timing their orbits, in theory, can be used to calculate longitude. And, as you know, that is what we're all looking for.'

Ah yes, Tom thought, longitude - the merchant philosopher's stone. Measure that and you could plot your position on any sea in the world, an incalculable commercial advantage.

'Elizabeth tells me Galileo came up with the idea some thirty years ago,' Ralph continued. 'But he couldn't take accurate sightings with his telescope on board a moving ship. You also need an accurate clock and there have been advances in these since his experiments. Elizabeth wants to try again and wondered if she could use one of our ships...'

He was interrupted by a shout from the back of the warehouse and, seconds later, their apprentice Sam Barnes ran into the room. 'Master Tallant, you have…oh good day Sir Ralph, I'm sorry to interrupt your conversation, but you must see this.'

The Tallant warehouse was located off Thames Street, near the river. Access was through a ginnel – a small arched tunnel that ran between and under the houses on the south of Thames Street, straight into the yard at the front of their premises.

Sam ran out of the warehouse, across the yard, and into the ginnel, Tom and his father following closely. The passage - wide enough for a two horse cart – was the route for all cargo from the Tallant warehouse to the busy streets of London. It was cold and damp and Tom coughed at the overpowering smell of piss. Their footsteps echoed along the cobble floor and arched ceiling but, as they approached the ginnel's end, the sound was drowned by the cacophony of street noise ahead.

Seconds later they were in Thames Street, surrounded by traders selling their wares. A grey haired woman carrying a tray of pies was yelling at the top of her voice, trying to avoid a small herd of sheep pushing past her, their shepherd whistling and calling to his dog. The landlord of the Swan with Two Necks stood outside his tavern shouting to passers-by, drumming up lunchtime trade while clearing the thick mud from his doorstep; and, above it all, was the constant hammering from sweating coopers in the barrel works opposite, pale sunlight glinting off their knee-length aprons as they fixed iron hoops onto wooden casks.

In the midst of this, Tom could see hundreds of people pushing and hugging each other, their cheering adding to the din trapped between the overhanging upper floors of the houses, shops and taverns.

'What madness is this?' Ralph Tallant shouted to his son, straining to be heard above the mayhem. 'When I arrived less than an hour ago, all was calm! At least they look happy!'

Sam grabbed the arm of a man who had stopped singing to swig beer from a tankard. 'What's happening, fellow? Why the celebrations?'

The man gaped at Sam. 'Haven't you heard? Where have you been? We've got him. We've finally got the bastard!' The man started singing and moving away. Sam pulled him back.

'Who? Who have you got?'

'Only Black Tom. Black Tom! Now we'll have his head!', the man shouted and ran into the crowd, swinging his now empty tankard

Tom glanced at his father who looked stricken. Ralph slowly returned down the ginnel, followed by the others, and stopped by the warehouse entrance. 'Sweet Jesus,' he murmured. 'He's given up Strafford. There is no reason to it. I was completely mistaken.'

'What are you saying, father?'

'Unless this is another infernal rumour infesting this city, our friends here are cock-a-hoop because the King must have signed the Bill that condemns the Earl of Strafford to execution,' he replied. He's caved in to the Commons.'

'But you said he gave his word to Strafford that he would be safe.' Tom continued. 'Strafford was his right hand man. The King had to save him...he gave his word! What message does this give to his enemies in Parliament?'

Ralph sniffed the air. 'Lord only knows, but this will only be the beginning. He may not know it, but Charles has just opened Pandora's Box.

'I feel a wrecking storm coming. And there'll be no sailing around it.'

Chapter 2

Bolton Hall, the Tallant family home

Tom rode up the driveway to Bolton Hall, and smiled at the sight of his family home.

The Hall was part of an Augustine Monastery broken up in King Henry's time. The chapel and dormitories were demolished, the stone taken by locals for building materials. But the abbot's house, refectory and cloisters had been saved and much altered by successive owners, to provide a comfortable home for the Tallants for the last 20 years.

It was a fine May morning and he could feel the heat of the sun starting to warm his back. He tethered his horse Meg at the stable wall and walked into the garden behind the house. A blackbird on a nearby meddler tree greeted his arrival with a tumbling waterfall of song, each refrain unique. He waved to Mark, the gardener, giving the lawn its first cut of the season with his scythe, then checked his saddlebag again. Yes, his precious cargo was still intact.

Tom approached a table under the ancient oak. His mother Beatrix Tallant was deep in conversation with Elizabeth and neither noticed him. He clutched the saddlebag to his chest.

'Good morrow to you both,' he called, bending to kiss them each lightly on the cheek.

'Ah, Tom!' his mother replied. 'Elizabeth and I are discussing herbs. She is proving most knowledgeable.' His mother struggled slightly with the pronunciation of the last word, a rare reminder that English was her second language. Beatrix Tallant came from a distinguished Dutch merchant family and had moved to England following her marriage to Ralph.

'Your mother has a wonderful collection of cooking herbs, but she wants to grow others that have healing powers,' Elizabeth explained. 'I have taken advice from Master Culpeper and we are deciding which to choose.'

Nicholas Culpeper. Tom frowned at the mention of the man. Culpeper was a leading member of the Coleman Street radicals and, to his eyes, dangerous company. Drawn together by their mutual interest in herbal medicine and addiction to tobacco consumption, Elizabeth had known Nicholas before meeting Tom, a thought that made him vulnerable and jealous.

She saw him frequently but insisted they were only good friends. Also, Culpeper had recently married, but Tom could not help himself. He regarded the herbalist as a rival for her affections, and decided to change the subject.

'Mother, I have a gift for you, delivered this morning to the warehouse, here in my saddlebag.' He reached inside and gently withdrew a small plant. It had a number of large leaves at its base with a single long stem topped by several clusters of dainty round flowers. Each had a delicate striping pattern coming from its centre.

Beatrix let out a little shriek. 'Oh my goodness. It's a Primula Auricula…and look! Its flowers have stripes! Where did you get it?

'A plantsman I know in the Royal Exchange is often sent new specimens from the Continent. I asked him to watch our for any auriculas.' He picked up the plant and inspected its small rosette flowers carefully. 'This little beauty arrived from Venice yesterday, so he sent it straight over.'

He carefully handed the plant to his mother who examined it closely. 'I had heard of this new variety but this is the first I have seen. I wonder if I will be able to grow more from it?'

'If anyone can, it will be you,' Elizabeth said. He smiled at her growing friendship with his mother. Their personalities were quite different but they had instinctively liked each other from their first meeting. They shared a love of nature, plants and flowers. When the Tallants bought the Hall, Beatrix inherited five acres of weeds and overgrown scrub, and proceeded to transform them into one of the finest private gardens in London. Elizabeth was now her keen student.

Tom sat at the table and stretched his legs. It was turning into a glorious day and he was glad to be out of London. Bolton Hall was located in the countryside north of Clerkenwell and seemed a million miles from the turmoil and anger currently surging through the capital. The public execution of the Earl of Strafford would take place tomorrow and a febrile atmosphere was building on the streets.

'My goodness, more visitors. What a busy morning.' Beatrix exclaimed. He looked up to see the unmistakable form of Barty Hopkins bustling towards them. In his wake, he could make out Robert Petty.

Tom met Sir Bartholomew Hopkins on his first day as a Member of Parliament and they soon became friends. Petty was an investigator for the Merchant Adventurers who he knew from a previous case, which had almost cost Petty his life, but thankfully he made a full recovery.

Slightly breathless, Barty wiped his brow, nodded at Tom and then bowed to his mother. 'Forgive this intrusion Lady Tallant. Wonderful to enjoy your glorious garden once more. And I think you know my companion Robert Petty?'

'Tis a great pleasure to see you again, Ma'am,' Petty replied and inclined his head towards Beatrix.

'This morning we visited the Tallant warehouse, seeking your son on an urgent matter,' Barty continued. 'Apparently he had left for Bolton Hall, so we set off in hot pursuit!'

'Well sit down Sir Bartholomew and take the weight off your feet,' Beatrix interjected. 'I'll leave you to your business and make myself useful. First on the list is putting my new plant in a larger pot. Elizabeth, thank you so much for your invaluable advice on expanding my herb garden. Much food for thought. ' And with that she walked towards the house clutching her precious Primula Auricula.

'So, what news from the City?' Tom asked. 'Presumably in a fever over tomorrow's execution?'

Barty nodded vigorously. 'I hear wild rumours at every street corner. Do you know the latest? The French are planning to invade to save Strafford! Complete lunacy. And speaking of the French, the Queen Mother has been waylaid and jostled in her coach and now guards are posted at St James Palace. Thousands will flock to Tower Hill tomorrow, but not me.'

'A wise decision, given you both declined to sign Strafford's death warrant,' Robert Petty commented. Barty and Tom had refused to support the Parliamentary Bill of Attainder that had sealed the Earl's fate. As a result, their names were included on a list of dissenters posted throughout the city by the King's enemies to stir up trouble.

'The case against him was not sound,' Tom replied. 'To me, his guilt was not proven. The Bill was a desperate and dishonest device by the Puritan junto to rid them of Strafford because the mob demanded it. I could not sign it.'

'Me neither,' Barty added. 'However, I doubt if a gang of Apprentice Boys on the rampage would recognise me if they fell over me. Anyway, we have something even more urgent to deal with. Robert and I are wrestling with a complete mystery and we need your advice urgently. It is a matter of the greatest secrecy,' and, at that, he glanced at Elizabeth.

'Anything you tell me can also be said to Elizabeth. Her

powers of deduction might assist you.'

Barty glanced at Petty who nodded. 'Err...very well, if you say so. But what I am about to tell you cannot be repeated to anyone, as you will soon understand. Robert, perhaps you would like to explain?'

He studied Petty. Those dark brown eyes the colour of weathered oak. That same inscrutable expression. He had come to trust Robert Petty but had also experienced the sharp end of Petty's investigative powers. He would be a formidable enemy should you fall foul of him.

'I have been investigating a case of murder on the waterfront, and now a second person has disappeared. I believe the two incidents may be connected,' Petty explained, his eyes searching Tom's face for any reaction. He had learned this was one of Petty's interrogation techniques and so averted his gaze, instead admiring a clump of blue columbines flowering near his seat.

'Two weeks ago, a dead man was fished out of the Thames. He had been stabbed in the chest. Through our contacts, we have identified him as Geoffrey Aston. Now a second person, Francis Cavendish, has gone missing.' Petty paused. Barty looked uncomfortable, squeezing his hands together.

'May I ask if you're investigating this on behalf of the Merchant Adventurers,' Tom enquired.

Petty paused. 'No, I am not. We are pursuing the matter in a personal capacity.' There was another pause, leaving Petty's words heavy in the air.

'You must excuse me gentlemen,' Elizabeth intervened. 'It appears we may be here a little while, so I hope you will not object to me filling a pipe?' And before anyone could reply, she pulled a small pouch of tobacco and clay pipe from her cloak pocket, which she proceeded to fill rapidly. She dipped again into her cloak, withdrawing a piece of polished glass. Barty was staring at her while Petty raised a quizzical eyebrow as she held the small glass encased in a ring of brass up to the sun breaking through the cloud, and gently tilted it back and forwards.

A white spot of light appeared in the bowl of the pipe and, seconds later, as Elizabeth drew on the stem, a spiral of smoke began to rise from the tobacco. 'Well, goodness me,' Barty exclaimed and she sat back and drew on the pipe, with a look of contentment. Petty studied her closely then shook his head slightly and smiled. This was one of her party pieces that Tom had seen many times, but he still enjoyed the reaction of those who witnessed it.

'So, where were we gentlemen?' Tom continued. 'You want our help with a matter you are both pursuing in a personal capacity? And, as you say, the circumstances require complete confidentiality?' Barty nodded vigorously.

He reflected on the relationship between his two friends. On the face of it, there was little to draw them together – a Member of Parliament and an investigator. Except both were Catholics and that forged a secret and unshakable bond between them. London was currently gripped with hysteria about alleged papist plots and sedition, a dangerous time to be a practicing Catholic or provide them with assistance.

Tom had previously shared this knowledge with Elizabeth. Both knew that, just by having this conversation, they were entering dangerous waters. 'Was there anything special about this man Geoffrey Aston, that I need to know?'

Bertie sighed. 'He was a Jesuit priest, as is Francis Cavendish.'

Tom took a sharp intake of breath and glanced at Elizabeth, whose face was impassive. Even though the garden was empty, he lowered his voice. 'You've lost two Jesuit priests! I didn't realise that many were still in England.'

'There are more than you know,' Petty replied. 'Smuggled in

from France to travel the country taking mass, which only a priest can do. They hide in a network of safe houses across London and outside.'

'Which you help with,' Tom interrupted. Silence, again. 'Gentlemen, if you want my...our assistance, we need to know exactly what we are getting into. And why you have come to me.'

'The last known hiding place for Cavendish was near Billingsgate,' Barty explained.

'Close to my warehouse,' he said flatly.

'Exactly,' Petty added, 'in an old building used as a temporary hide for those requiring access to the river, presumably for a quick escape.'

'So you're hoping Tom will make discreet enquiries to establish if anyone was seen on the night in question?' Elizabeth interjected. Barty opened his mouth to reply but she continued. 'For that to be a meaningful request, there must have been something distinctive or unusual in the physical appearance of this priest Cavendish, as I assume he was not wearing his cassock and hat?'

A smile played around Robert Petty's mouth. 'Quite so, Miss Seymour. At the time he disappeared the priest was dressed in an unremarkable fashion. However, he has flame red hair.'

'The fact it was not dyed an equally unremarkable colour suggests he left his previous hiding place in a hurry?' Petty and Barty said nothing.

'Just checking,' she added and, giving Tom a meaningful look, proceeded to re-fill her pipe.

'So, let's be clear,' Tom continued. 'This 'favour' you seek will require me to ask questions in my neighbourhood that will prove I know Francis Cavendish, or at least his appearance, at a time when it will be crawling with the anti-papists hot on his trail?'

Barty wriggled on his chair, wringing his hands. 'Oh dear. When you put it like that...' and he shot Elizabeth a glance. 'Forgive me Tom. What you say is true but we are desperate to find Cavendish before the authorities do. However, if it is asking too much, I understand.'

Tom studied the pair and felt his resolve weakening, but not because of Barty's pleading expression. It was Robert Petty's steady gaze, and the knowledge that he had previously risked his life to help Tom. Nevertheless, he would be sticking his hand into a hornet's nest. He exhaled slowly and considered. Yes, there was one possible way forward.

'As it happens gentlemen, I do know someone who might be able to help. It will just be a matter of trying to persuade him.'

Chapter 3

The Tallant warehouse

Tom stood at the back of the warehouse and surveyed the River Thames. A warm breeze ruffled the surface of the water, sparkling in the morning sun. Seagulls arced across an azure blue sky, their familiar cawing cry competing with frequent shouts of 'oars' and 'sculls'. The boatmen were out, selling their services to travellers along and across London's busy waterway.

To his left, downriver, stood the forbidding presence of the Tower of London. Could the Earl of Strafford see or hear any of this from his cell? What despair must he feel, knowing this wonderful day would soon be taken from him by the axe?

He returned to a stock check he was conducting with Sam. Ships returning from the Bay of Biscay had reported storms, delaying the large spice shipments from the East. As a result, the price of pepper had risen at the Royal Exchange, a good opportunity for the Tallants to sell a portion of their reserves.

But the river was never far from his mind. Once again he went to scan the water, shielding his eyes from its bright reflection. He was looking for a particular boat but Jonah Dibdin was nowhere to be seen. He was renowned as one of the most skilled yet mean-spirited boatmen on the Thames. His lack of social graces was tolerated because he was the fastest, or so he said, and seeing him at work it was hard to disagree. Tom would hire him whenever possible and, knowing this, Dibdin would frequently pass by the landing stage at the Tallant warehouse. But not today.

Isaac stepped out of the warehouse and joined Tom on the wharf. 'A fair day, Master Thomas. Are you looking for someone?'

'Jonah Dibdin. He seems to have disappeared just when I need

21

him.'

The warehouse manager pointed to London Bridge, which straddled the Thames to their right. 'Well, there's your answer, master.'

The bridge and the houses lining its length were bathed in the morning sun. In several places gaps appeared where buildings had previously collapsed or been destroyed by fire, revealing people, horses and carts moving in a busy, two-way flow. However, today, almost all the traffic was coming from the south bank, moving slowly.

'Of course,' Tom exclaimed. 'They're going to Tower Hill for Strafford's execution. Jonah will be busy shipping people across.'

'Aye, you won't see him all day, except when the axeman's doing his work. Most boatmen will take a break then, but not Dibdin. He can row all day and will be looking for more fares. He'll be back.'

And so it proved. Early in the afternoon, Tom heard a familiar call at the rear of the warehouse. He waved to Dibdin on the water who, in one fluid movement, changed course and darted towards him.

'Oh it's you,' Dibdin said, reaching out for the side of the wharf. 'Where do you want to go?' This was Jonah's usual greeting and Tom had learned to ignore the disappointed tone.

'I'm not looking for transport today. Just some of your unrivalled knowledge of the river.'

Jonah let out a mirthless laugh and leant over to spit in the water. 'Fine words but they won't pay my bread. While I'm sitting here blabbing to you, I'm losing fares. Now why should I do that?'

'Because I will reward you well enough if you find the information I seek. Shall I continue, or look for someone else?'

This was the courtship that Dibdin demanded. Tom had to curb his impatience, because Jonah always delivered.

'Alright, don't get all flustered. Tell us what you need, but make it quick,' Jonah retorted. So he explained about the missing man with red hair, omitting one crucial detail – that he was a Jesuit priest.

'Can you use your contacts on the river to find out if he's been seen? But do it quietly Jonah. There are probably bad people looking for this fellow.'

'I'm touched by your concern,' Jonah mocked. 'See what I can do.' And with that he pushed away from the wharf and, with a couple of powerful strokes surged back to the middle of the Thames.

By mid-afternoon, Tom had completed his stocktaking with a dozen sacks of pepper put aside for sale the following morning. He was arranging for a sample to be delivered to the Royal Exchange when his father burst through the warehouse entrance.

'Round up everyone. I think we will soon have company.'

'I thought you were attending Strafford's execution on Tower Hill', noticing his father was out of breath.

'I was. Extraordinary scenes. More people than I've ever seen gathered together. I was not an admirer of Strafford but the man showed courage and composure in his final moments, surrounded by such a press of enemies. I left as early as possible to get ahead of the crowds. They're pouring down Thames Street as I speak and the mood is ugly. Strafford's death has given the King's enemies the victory they need and their blood is up. The Apprentice Boys are spoiling for a fight, and heading in our direction.'

Tom sprinted across the yard to the ginnel. He could hear shouting and breaking glass and as he entered, the noise became louder. He emerged onto Thames Street to see a dozen burly lads turning over a cart full of hay, laughing and cheering while the driver protested in vain. The boys kicked the hay across the street to be trampled by the passing crowd. Several others picked up stones and threw them at nearby shops, sending their owners scurrying for cover. They were seeking targets and heading in his direction. He darted back into the tunnel and up to the warehouse. His father stood in the doorway with Isaac and Sam.

'Where's Andrew?' he shouted.

'He's locking Meg in the stable,' Sam replied. 'He'll be with us in a moment.'

Tom appraised the assembled team. His father had his sword and, although advancing in years, could still give a good account of himself. Isaac was clutching an old rusted halberd. He did not lack courage but his movement was limited by a crippling shoulder injury sustained on the loading wharf many years ago, which still caused him constant pain. Sam came from farming stock, not short of brute strength but neither blessed with fighting instinct. The groom Andrew Lamkin, now walking towards them, was only a lad. How would he react to a mob at their door? It would not be wise to test their strength in a hand-to-hand fight. They needed to bluff this out.

There was a commotion at the ginnel entrance and a group of Apprentice Boys tumbled into the yard, laughing and cuffing each other. They turned and, seeing the warehouse, became more wary, moving around the edges of the yard like a pack of feral dogs, sniffing new territory. More followed and soon a dozen faced Tom and the others.

Ralph spoke quietly. 'Spread out slowly and face them up. But don't say anything, and keep your hands where they can see them.' His voice was calm and his speech measured. He took a step forward and broke the brooding silence.

'Good day, lads. Prime weather for a stroll in the City? '

His words were met by a rumble of sneering laughter and curses. A group at the back started talking among themselves, passing a bottle around, each taking a swig. Some were carrying stones and makeshift clubs.

'Whatcha got in there, then?' one of them shouted, pointing at the warehouse. 'Fine wine and booty from your travels, eh?' This stirred the gang, and they stepped forward, pointing their fingers at Ralph and shouting insults. 'Gonna share some of that with us, are you, old man?' another shouted which sparked more jeers and cheering.

Tom could see they were working themselves up to launch a charge. His father motioned to him to come closer and whispered in his ear. 'Walk steadily to the warehouse and bring back whatever you can find to defend ourselves. Be as quick as you can.'

Ralph then stepped forward to distract them. 'Ah yes, jewels and silks from the Orient. That's what many of you expect, isn't it? If only it were so. There is very little here to interest you. Only sacks of herbs. And not a bottle of wine in sight!'

This seemed to confuse the gang who started to argue among themselves. He seized the advantage. 'Look, lads. I'm willing to take one of you inside and show you what I say is true, if the rest of you remain out here.'

That was his first mistake. The crowd started shouting again: 'it's a trap. Do you think we're stupid?' The mood changed again as they pushed forward. A bottle sailed through the air and smashed at his feet, just as Tom reappeared, wearing his sword and carrying a bailing hook and a handful of makeshift clubs – Sir Ralph's second mistake.

At the sight of the weapons, the Apprentice Boys howled in anger, cursing and pointing at Tom. 'Steady, lads!' Ralph shouted, as the makeshift weapons were distributed. 'Spread out in a line but don't get isolated.'

The gang was now within ten feet, goading and mocking the small force defending the warehouse. More faces appeared at the entrance of the ginnel. A burly youth broke ranks and walked towards Isaac. 'Look at you, stupid old crookback. You gonna stop me, huh? Come on, try it. I'll put you down,' he sneered. He leant forward, lowering his defence, to spit at Isaac, who didn't need a second invitation to reverse his halberd and ram its pole end into the boy's stomach. The apprentice doubled up and fell to the ground, puking and moaning. At the sight of this, the new arrivals shouted and pushed forward to join the mob that now numbered over 20. Individually, they started darting forward, probing the line for a weakness. Avoiding the swords of Tom and his father, they soon found one.

Andrew, armed with a wooden staff, looked terrified as two men approached him. One stepped forward, inviting a blow. He swiped at the man but fear made his movement stiff and hesitant. The second pounced and grabbed the stave, then the two of them started pulling him towards them.

Isaac yelled at Andrew to let go, but he was frozen by fear. Within seconds two more joined in and he was jerked off his feet. The men dropped the stave and fell on Andrew, kicking and punching. Sam stepped in to help him and the defences were broken.

'Dear God,' Tom thought, as Andrew and Sam disappeared under a pile of bodies. 'They have us now.' He moved forward with his sword fully extended, shouting at the baying crowd at the top of his voice. He glanced over his shoulder and saw his father doing the same, but soon they would be surrounded, and then what? He winced as a stone hit his leg. The threat of Isaac's halberd had cleared the crowd from Andrew, who was now lying motionless on the floor. Sam was back on his feet, blood running from a head wound.

The Apprentice Boys backed off and then, scenting blood, pushed forward again, shouting and screaming. 'We can't take much more of this,' Tom realised, now fearful for their lives. He surveyed the sea of faces, contorted with rage, and then heard a distant whistle. Twice.

A pain shot though his head, a flash of light and he found himself prone on the floor, dazed, his father's voice shouting: 'Tom! Are you alright?'

He raised his head from the ground and leaning on his elbow, saw a stone by his feet, smeared with blood. He watched the mob, steeling himself to be overwhelmed, but then his confusion was complete. They were stepping back, returning to the entrance of the ginnel.

He shook his head, which hurt like the devil, and pulled himself to his feet. Yes, the gang was retreating. He couldn't understand. They were at their mercy.

He staggered towards his father who was staring at the entrance to the tunnel. Tom followed his gaze and saw a familiar face. 'Is that Peter?'

Ralph nodded and held his arm. 'No, don't greet your brother. Don't move.'

He watched as the disgruntled Apprentice Boys filed out of the yard, past his brother Peter, and back to Thames Street. Peter continued to watch and gave a slight nod before disappearing into the ginnel with the last of the gang. The yard which, minutes earlier, had been brimming with violence and fear was once again calm and empty.

'Did I hear a whistle?' Tom asked Ralph.

'Yes. Peter calling off his dogs. Just in time,' he added, looking towards Andrew, now sitting up holding his side. 'But that hunting pack must not discover he knows us. If they did, he'd be finished.

Chapter 4

Wapping Stairs

The Thames had reached low tide, exposing a narrow shoreline at Wapping Stairs. Tom was crouching on shingle between two posts covered in dripping weed, which were supporting the floor of the wharf above their heads. The body of a man was lying in front of him, face down. Only the feet were visible from the wharf above, but that had been enough for Jonah Dibdin,

The dead man's hair was matted with sand but there was no mistaking its bright red colour, and the contrast with his grey, turgid flesh. Jonah shuffled into place alongside him. 'Is this who you were looking for?',

'I think so, Jonah. How did you find him?'

'You said your man was hunted by the wrong sort, so it was short odds he'd end up in the river. If they dropped him near Billingsgate, with the tides and currents this time of year, he'd likely turn up around Wapping bend. So I've been keeping an eye out around here.'

There was a shout from above. He peered out from beneath the wharf to see the face of Robert Petty looking down at them. 'I fear we have found your missing person, Robert.' Petty said nothing but disappeared from view. Tom ducked back to rejoin Jonah.

'They always make the same mistake,' the boatman continued, 'loading the body with too much weight. If you want someone to disappear in the spring tides, drop them further down stream, nice and light, and they'll be feeding the fishes past Tilbury the next day.'

The dead man's thin cloak was still tied around his neck. Jonah carefully untangled the folds of cloth and examined the its pocket, which was torn away. 'There you go. This pocket was filled with weight, enough to sink him where he was dropped. After being dragged along the bottom for a few tides, the weight rips the pocket open, the rocks are lost and the body rises nearer to the surface, just as the tide's on its way out, and is left stranded here.

'Well, thank you for letting me know so quickly Jonah.'

'Had to. Spotted him first light. Another half hour and he'd be gone. So I sent word to you right away.'

'What? The tides would be in that quickly?'

Jonah gave him a pitying look. 'Not the tides. The snatchers. They get a good price from the medical men for a fresh piece of flesh, even soused in water.'

He heard footsteps crunching on the shingle and Robert Petty appeared at his shoulder. Together, they turned the body over. It was stiff and marble cold to the touch, the skin swollen and slick. The man's pale sightless eyes stared at the wharf above them, through strands of knotted red hair. Petty sighed and, out of Jonah's view, quickly crossed himself.

'I never met Cavendish,' he explained, 'but from his description, that's him.'

They examined the body and soon discovered a neat, pale hole punched in the victim's chest between the ribcage. Jonah gave a low whistle. 'Don't need to look any further. That's no nonsense, there. No nonsense at all. Single strike, in and up. Whoever did that, they don't know their tides but they can handle a blade, no doubting it.'

Petty nodded and climbed out from under the wharf followed by the others. 'Can you get rid of your man, Tallant?' he said quietly before moving away from the wharf to look across the river.

He turned to Dibdin. 'Thank you for finding him, Jonah. This is for your trouble' and he handed him a shilling .

Dibdin pocketed the coin and turned to go. 'Always a pleasure to do business. Let me know if you lose any more gentlemen.' and he loped off towards his boat, his powerful rowing shoulders dwarfing the rest of his body.

Tom joined Petty by the water's edge. 'Is it the same as the first death?'

'Exactly. Single stab wound to the chest. We'll examine him in more detail but your man's right. Francis Cavendish wasn't simply killed. He was executed, deliberately and expertly, not during a scuffle in a back alley. Then he was taken out on the water and dumped.'

Robert Petty's dark brown eyes rarely betrayed emotion. But at that moment Tom could see something. Was it anger? No, much more than that. The investigator was struggling to contain within him a deep fury.

'I'm sorry Robert. It is appalling that someone should be killed for their religious beliefs.'

'But was it that?' Petty replied. 'Catholics are murdered across Europe every day usually by one of two ways. Caught by the mob and slaughtered where they stand, or tracked down by the authorities and sentenced to death. This was neither. There was nothing judicial about it, but neither was it casual or random.'

Petty looked again at the river, now busy with boats of all sizes. 'They regard us as vermin. So why go to so much trouble, simply to kill another rat?'

Chapter 5

The Bolt and Tunn Inn, Alsatia

Will Jackson turned off Fleet Street into a narrow alley leading to the river. He was entering Whitefriars, now also know as Alsatia, a safe haven for London's criminals and a place to be avoided whenever possible.

It was formerly the site of a Carmelite monastery. The priory had long gone but the law of Church, not State, had remained from Fleet Street to the Thames. Hundreds fleeing justice moved in and violently repelled any attempt by the authorities to close their haven. As a result, in Alsatia there was no longer any law.

Will walked quickly down the alley and was relieved to see the distinctive sign of the Bolt and Tunn Inn – a barrel pierced by a crossbow arrow. He paused at the entrance, checking the path back to Fleet Street to his left, then down the way he had been heading to the river. All was clear, so he ducked through the low doorway and disappeared from view.

The tavern was quiet, with only a handful of regulars at rough tables near the serving counter. The smell of stale ale and tobacco hung thick in the air. A familiar anxiety descended as Will approached the landlord, a thick set man with tattoos covering his face, neck and forearms. Once again, he had been drawn to the lair of the beast by the voracious knot of hunger gnawing at his stomach. He had to continue, but would be a fool not to be afraid. One word out of place could seal his fate.

'Is he in?'

The landlord turned and considered William with a stony expression. 'What's your business?' he wheezed, his voice deep and breathy, caused by the broken nose flat on his face.

'I have information he will value.'

The landlord grunted and disappeared into a room behind the serving area. Will could hear low voices, then the landlord returned and beckoned him to enter. He took a deep breath as he walked into a darkened room and, through swirling tobacco smoke, saw the silhouette of a large man sitting with his back against the only window. The door closed behind him and Will remained silent. Not his place to start a conversation with Jack Dancer.

The large man removed his pipe from his mouth and released a prolonged, hacking cough, spitting noisily on the floor. 'So, little Will. Why have you disturbed my contemplations on this fine May morning? It must be something important.'

Will swallowed hard. His every instinct told him to turn and run, not stopping until he reached the other side of London. But it was too late for that. He had disturbed the beast and was now the centre of his fearful attention.

'Begging your pardon Jack…' Will cursed his timidity as he saw a sneer growing on Dancer's face. He must press on, deliver his prize. 'But I've found another for you. More papist scum.'

Dancer studied Will with his ice blue eyes, then took a draught from the tankard in front of him. 'Have you now? And who might that be, little Will?'

'A priest. In hiding, I'm told. North of Moorfields.' There. It was out. His treasured intelligence, all in a rush. Not how he had intended to play his hand. Once again he berated his fear of this man.

Dancer did not move, his expression blank. Will's heart sank. The silence was crushing him. Any thought of reward was fading by the empty second. Now he'd settle for escape. Finally the large man stood and approached him. Will flinched as Dancer put his burly arm around his shoulder and guided him towards the window. 'Well that's good news, my boy. Very good news. That makes me happy. But I am a little concerned about one thing - you said 'I'm told'.' Dancer stopped and spun him around. The smile had vanished. 'You wouldn't be feeding me any old wives' tales now, would you?'

Will winced as Dancer's iron grip tightened on his thin shoulder. He instinctively felt for the missing little finger on his left hand. Its loss was the price for wasting Dancer's time once before. 'No, no, Jack. I've got this from three different people, and two of them are people in his parish. This isn't tavern talk, I swear!'

Dancer relaxed his grip and turned with Will to the window once again. 'Good. That's what I like to hear. You see? You 're learning, aren't you, Will? A priest, you say?'

'Yes. And what's better is the people there have known him since he was a boy. They all grew up together in the parish. But they turned against him once he took up with papists. Now they want him out.' Relief had loosened Will's tongue and he was burbling again. He sensed Dancer's body stiffen and cursed himself for a third time.

Dancer's head dropped and he stared at the floor. 'Will, who did I say I was looking for?'

'You said priests. You said God had instructed you to rid us of these filthy papist priests.'

Dancer didn't look up. 'No, Will. I said I wanted *Jesuit* priests in hiding. So your man in Moorfields must be a Jesuit, otherwise you wouldn't be bothering me, would you? How long's he been a priest? How did he get his training if he's always lived in the parish?'

Will was struggling. 'They just told me he was a priest, well, learning to be one. That's why he's gone into hiding. He told them he was an acol...acoly...'

Dancer's shoulder sagged, and he slowly raised his head. 'An acolyte?'

Will nodded enthusiastically. 'Yeah, that's it. A filthy papist, like you said.

Jack Dancer sighed as he gripped Will's coat and effortlessly lifted him off his feet with a single hand. He looked to the ceiling, his voice pleading: 'Why do they not listen? Why make me do this?', and his head butted Will's face repeatedly, his voice ascending to a roar with each impact. 'An acolyte...is a fucking… apprentice… priest…you arseworm.'

It was over in seconds. Dancer stood, panting, Will hanging like a rag doll in his grip.

'I need Jesuit priests, not apprentices, Will. Not even parish priests who've taken Holy Orders. I need the top dogs. The missionaries. Have you got that? Eh?'

Dancer examined Will's destroyed face. There was no response. He grunted with disgust and dropped him on the floor. 'Billy, take this rubbish out and get me an ale.'

A giggle sounded in the gloom, from the corner of the room. 'You do 'em a service you know that, Jack Dancer. You really do.'

Chapter 6

Old Palace Yard, Westminster

The grey sky released a sharp rain shower as Thomas and his brother Peter stepped from the entrance of St. Stephen's Chapel into the Old Palace Yard.

The House of Commons had completed yet another busy sitting, the latest of many, as John Pym pushed through reforms to weaken the King and strengthen his Puritan cabal. Tom had arranged to meet Peter in the lobby afterwards and, after such a lengthy session he needed refreshment.

The two brothers hurried out of the Yard to the nearby Bull Inn and, once inside, found seats in a corner near the fire, and Tom ordered pottage and ale

'Peter, I wanted to see you first and foremost to thank you for your intervention outside the warehouse.'

Peter was momentarily bemused but then remembered: 'Oh that! I'm afraid the Apprentice Boys forget themselves from time to time, and become a little overheated. I'm glad I was on hand to bring them to heel.'

'So was I. It was about to turn very nasty. Someone could have been killed.'

'I'm not sure about that! You must understand, passions are running high on the streets. My brethren suffer insults and hatred each day. As Puritans, we see evil everywhere. It is understandable if some become angry.'

'Well, whatever you say, I was very grateful you appeared at that particular moment.'

'We must continue to oppose the King's attempts to meddle

with our religion, but I would never let any of my family be harmed in the struggle. Fortunately, I have risen to a position of sufficient seniority that allows me protect you when I can. But I can't know everything and I urge you all to be vigilant, and if you see trouble, walk the other way.'

'You feel the tide is turning here?'

'The signs are clear. When I returned from New England, I realised this country was changing, and so it has continued. Archbishop Laud and his odious reforms are in retreat and the Puritan voice can finally be truly heard in Parliament.'

Tom considered his brother. Seven years ago Peter had been introduced to the teachings of John Calvin by his Dutch uncle. Peter had seized on Calvin's belief that only a pre-ordained few were destined to enter the Kingdom of Heaven. By his twenty fourth birthday Peter Tallant was convinced that he was one of the chosen. From that day, his life was devoted to joining with others like him to form communities where they could live as they believed God had ordained.

'One day I will return to New England for good, but for the moment my place is here. I can carry the fight to the ungodly in this very city and ensure the victory to come, bringing an end to our persecution.'

'Now you sound like a Catholic!' he laughed. 'If you really want to know persecution, be a Jesuit! God's Bones, what has this country come to? Is nobody safe to worship as they wish?'

'We have to follow God's word, wherever it may take us,' Peter responded, his voice becoming strident. 'As the Lord said: Get thee out of thy country, and from thy kindred and from they father's house, unto the land that I shall show thee.'

Tom leant forward with a sigh. 'Come here, brother' and he hugged Peter hard, slapping him on the back.

A familiar face appeared by their side. 'Father! Good to see you', Peter exclaimed.

Ralph gave Peter another hug, and sat at their table. 'I have escaped your mother's shopping expedition, so thought I would join you briefly.'

'I told father I would be here with you when the Commons session finished.'

'Well, I'm glad you came now as I only planned a brief meeting with Tom. I must leave in a few minutes for an important session of our church council.'

'That's a pity, but I know you are busy. Has your brother passed on my thanks for your help outside our warehouse?'

'Yes he has, and I explained that feelings are running a little high but I was happy to be there to restore order. And talking of which...'

The sound of raised voices and then a cry of pain came from outside. They left their table and walked into the street to find two men fighting. One was taller and appeared to have the upper hand, landing a heavy punch that knocked his opponent to one knee. The taller man then aimed a kick but the grounded man grabbed his foot and hauled him over. Papers fluttered from his bag to join others strewn across the ground.

'Stop that!' Peter shouted. 'Desist!'

The two men turned to see the three Tallants walking towards them. They scrabbled to their feet and ran off in opposite directions. Ralph picked up the sheets of paper. 'Hah, political pamphlets. I should have known it', he exclaimed, scanning the papers in his hands. 'I have two here, one describing the execution of the Earl of Strafford in grisly detail. The other is the usual driveling nonsense about another supposed papist plot to blow up the Commons.'

'Well, it appears I have once more been called upon to do my civic duty, keeping the peace, but now I must be off.' Peter said. 'I'm sorry it's been such a fleeting meeting father, but trust I will see you soon. Give my love to mother and Ellen,' and with one more embrace, Peter was gone.

Ralph and Tom walked back into the tavern and returned to their table.

'Have you noticed how brazen they have become?' his father asked.

'The pamphlet sellers?' he replied. 'Yes, they seem to have lost their old furtive ways. No more pulling you into a corner and producing their wares from a secret cloak pocket. I've never seen them so near the Commons.'

'I thought it would happen when Pym abolished the Star Chamber, but not this quickly. With the power of the censor removed, the Stationers' Office has lost its teeth. Dozens more presses are setting up across London as we speak. And now they are fighting over the best places to pedal their lies!'

'Are you sure it is all lies?' Tom asked and held up a news sheet he had recovered from the tussle.

'Well I never,' Ralph exclaimed, his scowl transformed into a grin. 'A pamphlet that is in *favour* of the King! Saying he is in Scotland, calming their fears over his religious reforms. Now that's more like it. You see? Freedom to publish can cut both ways. The King's supporters are finally realizing the importance of public opinion. They're making their voice heard.'

'I feel it in Parliament also. The wind is changing direction. I say it softly, but resistance to John Pym and his cabal may be growing. They have been unstoppable in recent months in their drive to make the King abandon Strafford. But his death has woken some from their dream, or should I say this nightmare. Now they're shouting 'Enough!'

'Look how Pym is being thwarted in his attempt to remove the bishops from the Lords,' Ralph responded. 'He knows their votes are blocking his reforms, but they have said: 'No. We do not want any further change'. I am not always fulsome in my praise of his lordships but, on this occasion, I applaud them!'

Tom considered the Lords, the two pamphleteers fighting in the street and the angry mob who attacked the warehouse. Battle lines were being drawn. And that would benefit nobody.

His thoughts were disturbed by Andrew Lamkin who pushed through the door of the tavern and ran towards their table. He gave a hurried bow to Tom's father.

'Begging your pardon, Sir Ralph. Lady Beatrix told me where to find you. It's Bolton Hall, sir. You've been robbed…and the house proper turned over!'

Chapter 7

Bolton Hall

Tom picked up the shattered remains of a Delft plate, a present to his mother from Uncle Jonas in Amsterdam, now broken beyond repair. He surveyed the wreckage in his parents' living room - tables upended, chairs broken, cupboards prised open, contents strewn across the floor.

His father strode in, his face tight with fury. 'It's the same in every room. Even your mother's glass house has been ransacked, her plants scattered everywhere.' He was struggling to retain his composure.

'How is she?'

'Not saying much. She feels violated. When I discover who is responsible, and I will, they will sorely regret this wanton destruction.'

Tom picked up his mother's shawl and walked into the garden. Beatrix was sitting on a bench staring at a broken plant, the Venetian primula he had given her. He placed the shawl around her shoulders and sat next to her. 'Mother, this is terrible. I'm so sorry. Are you hurt?'

Beatrix Tallant looked at the damage and shook her head. 'In my heart, yes, but otherwise intact. Thankfully we were not here when our unwelcome visitors arrived.'

'What happened?'

'We're still trying to find out from the staff. One or two have been beaten quite badly. Your father has sent for Robert Petty. We're hoping he can find whoever is responsible,'

'Oh my God. What about Ellen?' Tom said with a start.

40

'Visiting friends, thank goodness. She's on her way home. This could be her now...' Beatrix continued, turning her head towards the sound of voices coming from the house.

But it was Elizabeth, striding across the lawn towards them, her arms outstretched. She embraced Beatrix and stood back to examine her. 'Sir Ralph has told me what has happened, Lady Beatrix. If I may suggest, you should be inside after such an alarm. You could get a chill.'

Beatrix shook her head. 'There is nowhere to go. They have ruined every room. I'm not ready to see it again.'

'Will you come to my parents' house? It won't take two minutes in our coach. It's here, waiting in your drive. You can stay while Bolton Hall is restored to some order.'

Tom appreciated Elizabeth's kind offer but thought it would be politely declined. However, Beatrix nodded and reaching over to hug her, the tears finally came, coursing silently down her face. He mouthed his thanks to Elizabeth who gently guided Beatrix to the driveway. Then he headed for the kitchen where he found the cook, bathing Mark's face, her hands shaking as she gently wiped crusted blood from his nose and mouth. His left eye was heavily swollen and already half shut, and he was pressing a cloth inside the front of his mouth.

'Loose teeth?' Tom asked. Mark nodded. 'Don't speak then. Let me talk to Cook, when she's finished cleaning you up.' He walked into the pantry and opened the tap of an ale barrel. Filling three mugs, he returned to the kitchen, placing two on a table. 'Mark, here's some ale if you can manage it. Cook, you need to drink this too.'

He righted an upturned stool and sat by the kitchen hearth. Usually its fire gave off a fearsome heat but today it had been left untended since early morning. He raked the glowing embers in the grate and added fresh kindling and timber from the log pile. Within minutes, flames were licking the brittle bark of the

41

crackling firewood, smoke and sparks disappearing up the broad chimney entrance.

Tom sat back and minutes later was joined by Cook. He told Mark to retire to his cot in the servants' quarters and rest his head, then let Cook slowly drink her ale.

'Does that feel better? Do you want another?' Cook shook her head. 'So, tell me what happened. Slowly, from the beginning.'

Twenty minutes later, he emerged from the kitchen to see his father talking to Robert Petty and Elizabeth. Order was slowly being restored as members of household put the furniture back into place. Anything beyond repair was being piled in the coach house.

'How is mother?'

'She is resting. I have given her a herbal draught to calm her and, if possible, help her sleep a little.' Ralph thanked Elizabeth as he led them to a table in the corner of the living room. As they sat, he nodded to Robert Petty to speak first.

'First Sir Ralph, may I express my outrage at the destruction of your property. I'm only glad that you and Lady Tallant were absent. You may wish you'd been here to repel the raiders and mete out summary punishment. But seeing the damage they have caused, I am relieved you were not.'

'You believe they would have harmed mother and father?' Tom asked.

'At first sight, it appears they were a desperate, violent and large force. You did well to miss them. Tom, you've had an opportunity to question one of our key witnesses? Good. So, let's pool our knowledge.'

Tom started first, recounting the cook's information, gathered from what she witnessed and what other staff had told her.

'About 30 minutes after father and mother left for London there was a knock at the front door. A young man stood alone. He was walking to the city and could he possibly have a drink of ale and a crust of bread, as he hadn't eaten for more than a day? This was not an unusual occurrence and staff knew the family would not turn someone from their door, if they were in need and appeared to be harmless.

'He was directed to the kitchen at the side of the house. As one of the kitchen maids walked into the yard with his food and drink, two other men appeared from behind a stack of barrels, jumped on the girl, one holding a knife to her throat. Both were wearing black hoods with eyeholes, covering their faces completely.

'They told Cook to let them in, or the maid would suffer. She had to agree. The man with the knife whistled loudly and another seven masked men walked into the yard and they entered the kitchen together. Within ten minutes all the staff were captured. Several, like Mark, put up a fight, but were overwhelmed by the force of numbers.

'The men tied the staff up in the kitchen. Two stayed to guard them while the rest proceeded to ransack the house. The staff could hear crashes as the gang moved from room to room. They didn't seem in a hurry. Eventually the noise stopped, there was a shout and the two guards left the kitchen. All remained quiet for some time, then one of the staff managed to free himself and raised the alarm.'

'Sir Ralph, may I now turn to you?' Petty said. 'Having inspected the damage, what are your initial thoughts on why the men raided your house and what they were looking for?'

'It appears that valuables have been taken – jewelry and silver plate- but these men were intent on destruction as much as theft. Several expensive pieces of furniture were broken up instead of stolen. Valuable paintings were also ignored. These were not professional thieves. I can only think some kind of a message was intended. Perhaps the gang were falsely informed we were supporters of the King, or even closet papists.'

'What about those people who tried to attack the warehouse?' Tom asked.

'Yes, of course, I had forgotten,' his father replied. 'Maybe they had unfinished business, wanted to teach us a lesson. And while they were about it, some couldn't resist pocketing the jewels and silver to make the trip into the country worthwhile. The current political unrest is causing all kinds of lawlessness.'

There was silence in the room. Petty turned to Tom's father, his voice lowered. 'If what you say is true Sir Ralph, this represents a new and very troubling phase of the current public unrest in London...for we're not *in* London. As I say, *if* true, the ambition of the mob is growing, and their range of targets with it.'

'What about your murder investigation? How is that progressing?' Tom asked. 'Do you think those killings could also be related to this mob?'

'Everything has gone quiet, I'm afraid. I have no new information to speak of but I'm inclined to agree with your boatman Dibdin. The red haired man we found on the foreshore at Wapping – his killing had all the hallmarks of a professional assassin, not an angry crowd. I will continue to pursue it, as well as today's attack on your family'.

The meeting ended and Tom wanted to check on his mother, so Elizabeth sent the coach back and together they followed on foot to her home nearby.

As they walked, a gentle breeze stirred the top of the Queen Anne's Lace lining the road's edge. Bright clumps of red campion peeped out from the foliage beneath. Elizabeth linked her arm with Tom as they strolled along, the sun warming their backs. He could smell her perfume of lavender and rose and once again wondered at her ability to create another world for him, within minutes of leaving the destruction at Bolton Hall. Why couldn't more of his life be like this?

They continued in silence for five minutes. Instinctively, neither wished to break the moment.

'You didn't speak at the meeting,' Tom finally observed.

'There were a lot of questions on my mind'.

'About what? The events at Bolton Hall?'

'Yes, of course. If what Robert Petty suspects is correct and the radical mob wanted to make their mark outside London, why choose Bolton Hall? Your parents are not known as rabid royalists. There are many more obvious targets.'

'Maybe those places are better defended for that very reason, or situated in more public places, nearer the city,' Tom replied. 'Bolton Hall is more of a backwater. Less chance of being disturbed. And it could be the same gang we encountered at the warehouse, with a point to prove. I've even been thinking perhaps our house was attacked because I refused to sign the Bill of Attainder that condemned Strafford to death. That could also explain why that gang came the warehouse. The word is about; and I'm known for my friendship with Barty, a King's man, who also didn't sign.'

'Well that could be another reason,' Elizabeth calmly replied. 'Still, I am not convinced. There's something nagging in the back of my mind. Something your father said a while ago but I can't put my finger on it. Anyway, let us see what Mr. Petty's enquiries uncover. Of course, a certain person I am visiting next week might have a view. '

He could tell she was bursting to share her news. 'So who is that – someone important?'

'No, not really. Only the Countess of Carlisle.'

'Lucy Carlisle, formerly the Earl of Strafford's mistress?'

'Now hush. I'm surprised at you! That's just court gossip.

'But why on earth would Lucy Carlisle want you?'

'Tom! How deeply hurtful. A lady of my talents, there could be many things. Maybe she wants to know where to buy the best

Virginian tobacco.'

They both burst out laughing which subsided, once again, into silence.

'No doubt I will find out when I see her, but one thing's for sure.' Elizabeth added. 'There'll be no time for dizzy wits or she'll have me for breakfast.'

Chapter 8

Little Salisbury House, Strand

A rustle of fabric made Elizabeth turn to see the Countess of Carlisle enter the room. Lucy Carlisle, the royal courtier famed throughout England, was standing before her. Try as she might, she could not suppress a feeling of nervousness and, to her dismay, a certain deference.

'The Countess stepped forward to greet her. 'How good of you to come! I have looked forward to our meeting very much.' She doubted that, but Lucy Carlisle was renowned as much for her charm as her beauty. She must want something, Elizabeth concluded, but for the life of her she could not imagine what.

'Let us it sit by the window. There is such a wonderful view of the garden and the river beyond, don't you think? Would you like some refreshment?'

Elizabeth politely declined and followed her host to the end of the room where they settled into two exquisite reception chairs. Probably French and absurdly expensive. To keep the enveloping sense of unreality at bay, she calculated the price of one seat and realised it would keep her in tobacco for a year. She pinched her leg, as she accepted Lucy's invitation to sit. I'm in the presence of the she-wolf. Must keep alert.

'So, here we are,' Lucy said. 'How pleasant.'

She studied her host. Her dress was dazzling in aquamarine silk, with an embroidered petticoat studded with perfect small sapphires. She was now past her fortieth year but, despite the first hints of a double chin, the Countess retained sufficient confidence in her appearance to wear a low cut bodice, set off by a spectacular pearl necklace. Her hair was also a la mode, surrounding her face with tight pale brown curls.

If not a work of art, her appearance was the result of much consideration. Her eyes, her smile, even her exquisite smell, matched by her jewel encrusted clothes created a shimmering presence and, once again, Elizabeth felt herself drawn in. She had wondered if Lucy would be in black, so soon after the death of her very close friend, the Earl of Strafford. But to do so would have confirmed the rumour that they had become lovers following the death of her husband the Earl of Carlisle five years ago. And showing her hand was not in Lucy's nature

'I am sure you will be busy, so I will get straight to the point. I believe you and I share a good friend.' Elizabeth's brow furrowed. The mystery was deepening.

'No?' Lucy continued. 'Well, how surprising. I'm sure you would not have forgotten him. Henry Jermyn is such a dashing fellow.'

Elizabeth was jolted out of her reverie. Now the reason for their meeting had her full and anxious attention. Henry Jermyn had fled England weeks earlier when his plan to release Strafford from the Tower was uncovered. She had learned to both fear and despise the man in the past and had offered up a silent prayer of thanks when he left the country.

'Ah, Mr. Jermyn, of course. I should have realised you would be known to each other,' she replied with a sardonic smile. 'But I haven't seen him in quite a time and now I hear he is abroad?'

'He has been treated most unfairly,' Lucy said with a childish pout that, in a breath, turned into a genteel sneer. 'His part in that scheme was completely overstated. But see how they twisted the truth to condemn my poor Strafford to the block. What else can you expect?'

Elizabeth had to tread carefully. Jermyn was the Queen's

favourite but now Her Majesty had been denied his company because of his attempt to free Strafford, Lucy's 'special' friend. This was not something Lucy would want the Queen to dwell upon.

'Before his hasty departure, Mr. Jermyn secured the King's agreement to appoint my brother-in-law the Earl of Leicester to the position of Lord Lieutenant of Ireland, to replace my fallen Strafford. He was a most accommodating fellow, and now he too has gone. It's too much, really,' and the stone face now shed a tear. Lucy was giving a full performance of her wiles at their first meeting. Should she feel flattered or was this Lady Carlisle's usual modus operandi?

'But Henry Jermyn has left me with one final gift – you!' Lucy smiled and clapped her hands with delight.

Elizabeth shrank into her chair, repulsed at the notion of being Jermyn's gift to give and Lucy Carlisle's to accept. This was no good. She must get on the front foot. 'Well, I am at your service, Lady Carlisle. How exactly can I help?'

The reception room was large with no one else present. Nevertheless, the Countess leaned forward and lowered her voice conspiratorially. 'What I will tell you must never be repeated, do you understand? Not under any circumstances.'

She nodded, not taking her eyes off Lucy Carlisle's face.

'Because of my previous long and loyal service as lady-in-waiting, I have won the Queen's confidence and earned her trust in all matters. Her Majesty plays a prominent role in the business of the nation and is a constant and valued advisor to our King, especially during these most challenging times. Our current travails take the King to many different parts of this island. Recently he was in Scotland to subdue those with rebellious intentions. In such circumstances, it is imperative that the flow of information between King and Queen continues uninterrupted, as affairs of state are currently in a delicate condition.' At last Elizabeth could see what was coming, and it filled her with misgivings.

'Their most gracious majesties require a unique system to encode their correspondence and it will be very much to my advantage if I can provide it. The cipher must be newly minted, unknown by any other than its creator. Henry Jermyn once told me he was confounded by a code that had defeated his best men, and you cracked it within a matter of hours. He could not speak highly enough of your talents. He assured me you would be both willing and able to create a cipher that would be safe and relatively easy to use.'

Elizabeth sighed. Damn Jermyn. She had only acquiesced to his request under duress, when he threatened to ruin her father's career in Whitehall. She must assume that threat remained, only now her father would be in the clutches of Lucy Carlisle.

The Countess fixed her with a sweet smile and eyes of steel. 'So, Elizabeth Seymour. I am giving you an opportunity to serve your King and Queen, in their time of need.'

'What say you?'

Chapter 9

The Bolt and Tunn Inn, Alsatia

Jack Dancer held up the gold bracelet to a shaft of sunlight penetrating the gloom. He turned it over, playing the light over a row of small rubies running down its centre.

'Hmm, pretty little piece,' he murmured and slipped it into his pocket before turning to a small pile of jewellery on the table. He glanced at the meagre haul in silence, save for the tapping of his knuckles on the tabletop. Dancer stepped back and sat down. He reached for his tankard and swallowed a long draught of beer. 'So, this is everything?'

Billy Boy fidgeted nervously in his usual place, a wooden stool in the corner of the room facing Jack. From the bitter experience of others, he had learned to keep two arms' length from his master at all times. The stool was a deliberate choice. Easy to vacate in a hurry, it also provided a useful obstacle should Jack make one of his unpredictable, venomous lunges. Such attention to detail kept Billy Boy alive and in his position of chief accomplice to Jack Dancer. He had lasted six months, twice as long as his predecessor, each day like living on the gallows with a rope around his neck, never knowing when the floor would disappear beneath him. But it had its compensations.

'There's also some silver plate. Nothing special. You told us not load ourselves with too much.'

'And this *is* everything? No-one tempted to lift a piece or two for themselves?'

'I got all the boys to turn out their pockets before we left the

Hall. I told them how you'd take it, if any tried it on. And they know not to say a word if they want to see another day.'

'Good. Well hopefully that will confuse the Tallants. Did we visit to rob the place or go on the rampage? It sounds like the lads enjoyed themselves!' and Dancer's face broke into a sour grin.

'We upended every room. Caused so much damage you couldn't have known we were looking for anything.'

Dancer's head jerked up and he fixed Billy Boy with a murderous glare. 'And, as far as anyone was concerned, you weren't looking, were you, except for the gems you pocketed.'

Billy instinctively half rose from his stool, ready to escape: 'No, no, Jack. Only the jewellery. That's what I told the lads. Find a few valuables and then enjoy yourselves with a bit of carnage at the Tallants' expense. But I was taking a good peep while they were having fun, following them, from room to room, keeping my eyes open for…anything else.'

Dancer leaned back and said nothing. He removed a long dagger from his belt and impaled the tabletop. 'And, let's just check one more time. You found nothing?'

Billy could feel the stare from his master's cold blue eyes burning through his brain. A spasm of panic twisted his gut. He was terrified of leaving a shred of doubt in Dancer's mind. His life could depend on it. 'Nothing. Nothing at all.' He heard his voice croak like a frog, as fear flooded his body.

Jack Dancer held his gaze and then turned away. ''Tis a pity. But not a surprise.'

'I still don't understand why we didn't raid the house when the Tallants were home and make 'em tell us where everything was?'

Dancer sighed and gave Billy a look of disdain. 'Because then they would know what we were looking for, wouldn't they?

And before we could blink , it would be shipped to their family in Amsterdam, for safekeeping. Then where would we be? No, we need to keep them guessing, but keep on searching.'

'And what about the Jesuits? Do we keep looking for them?'

'For the moment, let's keep that iron in the fire, Billy, as their eminences from the Inquisition might have put it. Also – don't be tempted to fence those jewels or silver plate. Bury them for now. Nothing can be traced back to us, do you understand? Nothing.'

Chapter 10

Bolton Hall

Ralph Tallant was not a small man, and unaccustomed to looking upwards towards anyone. So Tom was startled to see him overshadowed by two giants as together they walked into the garden at Bolton Hall.

He was sitting at a table with Elizabeth, Robert Petty and Barty by the spreading meddler tree full of new fruit. They had been called together by his father to review progress on the investigation into the attack on Bolton Hall.

'What ho, Tom. Good morrow one and all.' Ralph inclined his head to each in turn. 'Good of you to come. Let me introduce Dirck and Jan.' He pointed to each and then stopped. Have I got that the right way round? No? Oh well, we will all learn soon enough!'

Both men smiled and stepped forward, bowing towards Elizabeth and then the others. Identical twins, both six foot three inches with immensely powerful shoulders and hands the size of dinner plates.

'It appears we are living in increasingly uncertain and unstable times,' Ralph continued. 'There has been a number of threats and attacks on our staff and property and there could well be worse to come. So I have decided to call in reinforcements. My brother-in-law Jonas in Amsterdam has kindly agreed to the loan of two of his finest,' and here he presented the twin giants with a flourish. 'Both are skilled wharf men but also know how to handle themselves should trouble occur. I'm sure you will agree they are a valuable addition to our team. I will sleep a little easier knowing they are looking over us. For now, Dirck is to be based at the warehouse and Jan here at Bolton Hall.'

Tom noticed throughout that Dirck was whispering to his brother. He assumed Jan's knowledge of English was limited, so it was sensible to assign him to Bolton Hall. A month or two under the tutorship of his mother Beatrix would have him talking English like a native.

The twins were taken back to the house to continue their introductions while Ralph sat at the table with the others. 'Jonas tells me they're inseparable and always work, fight and play together. Unfortunately we need cover both here and on the river, so it will be interesting to see how they cope apart. Anyway, to business. Mr. Petty, have you made any progress with your investigation?'

'In a manner of speaking, Sir Ralph. The most noteworthy result is that I have virtually no new information.' Tom could see his father frown, but Elizabeth nodded her head. 'I have used all my usual contacts throughout the City and particularly along the river. Most hadn't heard about the robbery at Bolton Hall. A few were aware of a break-in, but didn't have any details, or any knowledge of who might be responsible.'

'And in your experience, Mr. Petty,' Elizabeth cut in, 'that is unusual, in fact barely credible?'

Petty nodded. 'Especially when the attack was so well planned and involved at least ten people. It tells me this was either the work of a gang from out of town, or the instigator is a man who has the power to silence a lot of voices in the City.'

'That's interesting' Ralph replied. 'After the attack, I asked my son Peter for his opinion, given his influence within the Puritan community. He surprised me. I expected a tongue lashing when I suggested godly radicals could be responsible. Instead he admitted there are a number of hot-heads among

Pym's junto and, for our own protection, we should not discount the possibility of their involvement. He was angry about what happened, both for our sakes and the damage it did to the Puritan cause, and said he would keep his ear to the ground.

'So it was political?' Tom interjected. 'Set up by Pym or one of his cronies? There can't be many more powerful people in the land at the moment than John Pym.'

'Well, I can't imagine anyone based a long distance away trying something like this,' Petty added. ' It would be almost impossible to bring a large group this close to London without attracting attention.'

'Quite so,' Elizabeth replied. 'That leaves Pym's Apprentice Boys but I do not imagine they are well suited to subterfuge and careful minute-by-minute planning. Don't they act more on instinct? Also, if they left London hell-bent on rampaging through Bolton Hall, and arrived only half of the hour after your parents left, why didn't their paths cross? They must have had extraordinary luck to remain undetected, or they weren't on the London road to Bolton Hall, which as we have discussed is unlikely and I...'

Ralph interrupted. 'Elizabeth, your ingenious mind is once again producing many valuable questions, but answer me this,' and here he coughed and softened his tone, 'if they were not Apprentice Boys, not politically motivated, they must have had theft in mind. So, if they went to so much trouble to plan this raid, with so many people involved, why did they spend more time damaging the house than looking for other valuables to steal? I grant you, the furniture would be difficult to carry back to London, but there were many things they ignored, for example a number of valuable miniatures in our collection of paintings.'

Petty now spoke up. 'And if they were thieves, why have they not sold their haul? I have spoken to a number of villains who buy stolen goods, and owe me a favour. None have seen any of the items from Bolton Hall on the market.

'As I thought' Ralph added. 'No, I'm sure I have damn Pym to thank for this. I don't know how yet, but I swear he will regret crossing swords with my family.'

Chapter 11

Bishop's Gate, East London

Elizabeth pulled the hood of her cloak tightly around her as she headed north up Bishop's Gate Street.

Londoners were up and about their business and the streets were crowded. The press on the wooden boardwalk kept forcing her on to the road, which resembled a midden more than a thoroughfare. It was like this throughout the city which was drowning under the weight of its growing population. People were dumping waste anywhere and everywhere, and the city's rudimentary sewage system was completely overwhelmed.

'Where will it all end?' she thought, stepping around a large heap of rubbish. Tom told her when the streets became a sea of mud and muck, the scavenger's carts could not reach the rotting heaps, which only made the problem worse. If it weren't for foraging kites that descended on anything freshly dumped, nothing would be cleared.

She avoided a putrid green slime seeping from the stinking pile. It was draining into a shallow gutter at the side of the street, where the slime was backing up against the rotting corpse of a rat. The smell was appalling.

Elizabeth wished she was still in her carriage but had told her coachman to drop her off at Bishop's Gate. Attacks on coaches were becoming fashionable in parts of London. Was the city really becoming so lawless? Only yesterday, she'd been told the Apprentice Boys had pulled the Lord Mayor off his horse.

That was the problem. Living in the countryside well beyond the City walls, she had to rely on second-hand information, which frustrated her scientific mind. She needed to see for herself how volatile the situation was. She knew who to ask and hoped they might also have the answer to another pressing question.

In her elegant cloak and fine shoes, she was attracting glances as she forged through the crowd on foot and was already regretting her decision to travel alone to Spitalfields. Tom was not available and she couldn't countenance asking her father. Perhaps her eagerness for research had taken her too far this time.

Twenty minutes later Elizabeth felt safer but tired and dirty. She had left behind the threatening crowds on the busy streets and was surrounded by smaller dwellings, kitchen gardens and fields. Her shoes were ruined and her legs ached. It was a relief when she saw the outline of St. Mary's Spital hospital ahead. As she entered its precincts, she took a moment to compose herself and adjust her cloak, but left its hood in place. To the left was a row of doors, the entrances to a collection of single floor dwellings. She walked to the end, knocked on the last and waited. She worried that the house might be empty and her difficult journey wasted, and was about to knock again when the door was opened.

'Elizabeth! How wonderful to see you.'

At once, she smelt the aroma of tobacco smoke and let out a sigh of relief. 'Nicholas, now that I have finally arrived, the pleasure is all mine.'

Nicholas Culpeper stepped forward, removing the large pipe clenched between his teeth, and peered out of the doorway. 'You've come alone? Was that wise?'

'Probably not, but I needed to see you urgently. Now let me in. I'm desperate for a smoke.'

The entrance to the house led directly into a small living room, furnished sparsely with a rough wooden table and two chairs. The distinctive smell of burning sea coal filled the room as a fire burned fiercely in the corner, its thick grey sulphurous fumes pulled swiftly into the chimney. She settled thankfully on a seat and carefully took a pipe and tobacco pouch from her cloak pocket. She filled the pipe and lit a taper as Nicholas fetched two mugs of small beer.

Both sat in silence for several minutes savouring the prime Virginian. They had met several years ago and Nicholas was the only person she knew whose passion for smoking matched hers.

'I wondered if you might not be at home, given all that's happening on the streets at present.'

Culpeper looked a little embarrassed. 'The truth is I was still lying a-bed until St. Mary's chimed ten.'

'You are not unwell, I hope?'

'Nothing a little restraint last night would not have put right.'

'Ah…what was the cause of your celebration?'

Culpeper paused to savour his news. 'We were toasting the success of my friend Alfred Brenner, who yesterday paid his compliments to the King, although I doubt his majesty welcomed Alfred's visitation.' Elizabeth waited. She knew her friend had a story to tell.

'A group of us was waiting on King Street. We knew Charles would be leaving Whitehall by coach for the House of Lords and aimed to shout some insults as he passed. We expected to be moved on by the Palace guards but none were to be seen. I thought our intelligence was faulty and we were wasting our time but, sure enough, a half hour later there was movement to our left and the King's coach came into view, mounted guards front and back.

'We were in a side alley and, as the coach neared, we stepped out onto King Street. Every moment I anticipated a hand on my shoulder or a pike in my back, but no, nothing. Once the horsemen at the front had passed, the King followed with only ten feet of fresh air between him and us. In a moment Alfred rushed forward with a shout, jumped on to the side of the coach and, leaning through the door window, threw a handful of pamphlets at the King.'

She sat with mouth open, smouldering pipe in hand. Her decision to travel on foot had been vindicated. Even royalty were not safe.

'Did he see the King? Did Charles say anything?'

'It happened so quickly. No time for conversation!' Culpeper laughed. 'But Alfred saw him well enough, pressed into a dark corner of the carriage, as far from the window as possible. He said the King looked neither startled or angry, just horrified!' Silence again, as Elizabeth digested everything she had heard. Her thoughts were interrupted by a sound in the distance, a percussive ripple followed by faint shouts.

'So I assume, if you were celebrating with Alfred last night, he must have made his escape?'

'We all did. Alfred stepped off the coach and we disappeared sharpish up the side alley. One of the horse guards bringing up the rear shouted at us, but no one followed. The handbills were freshly printed in Coleman Street that morning. The ink was probably still wet. They will have made interesting reading for the rest of the King's journey!' He started laughing and it turned into a wheezing cough. As it subsided, she again heard a crackling sound outside.

'Nicholas, I came today to get a first hand account of how bad the street disturbances are. Much of the information available to me is filtered through my family or the household servants, and I have this growing feeling I am sitting next to a giant keg of gunpowder without the slightest idea whether there is a fuse burning a path towards it. What brought this home to me was a recent shocking occurrence near to our house. You remember Thomas Tallant?'

'Your beau? How could I not, although I don't know what you see in him…'

'Nicholas. As you are so happily and recently married, I'm sure you have no interest in the nature of my relationship with Tom. Equally, I'm sure you will be interested, and disturbed to know, that a gang attacked his family home Bolton Hall and caused a great deal of damage.'

'Was anyone hurt?'

'One or two of the servants were roughed up quite badly but none of the family were at home. But every room is the house was turned over.'

'Anything stolen?'

'Only a few portable items such as jewels and silver plate. Because the destruction was so wanton, and relatively little taken, the Tallants wonder if the attack might have a political motive?'

'What? The Apprentice Boys going on the march to Clerkenwell, and beyond?' Nicholas guffawed. 'Not quite their style, I think. Not enough taverns on the way. No, I have not heard of any Puritan involvement in an attack on Bolton Hall, but I'm sorry for the Tallants' discomfort.'

They refilled their pipes then Nicholas gave her a rueful look. 'You know, I am a bit disappointed in you. You hear about a gang of hooligans breaking into a neighbour's house and you immediately think of the Apprentice Boys!' Culpeper paused and gazed out of the window. She could see excitement in his eyes as he returned his gaze to her. 'But if you want to witness the growing opposition to the King, and how serious it is, let me show you something.'

Nicholas led the way from his house and as they turned a corner into an open field, Elizabeth saw a large number of men in the distance lining up in rows, facing a tall and deep embankment of soil. As they approached, the front line stepped forward, holding muskets.

'Shooting practice for our local trained band,' Nicholas explained. As he spoke, there was a shouted command and the men raised their weapons as one. Another shout and puffs of smoke rose above the men followed immediately by a ripple of musket fire, the crackling sound she had heard in Nicholas's home. The line that fired then stepped back, handing their muskets to the next row to reload.

'Over a hundred meet in Spitalfields for drill practice and musket training twice a week. Weavers, watermen, butchers, and bakers - men of London, ready to defend their homes and their rights. As you can see, we haven't sufficient muskets yet for all, but they will come. It's finally happening! The people have had enough. The old deference is breaking down. We're too busy preparing ourselves for battle to go looting country houses. And if we wanted to make a show, we'd choose bigger targets, like the King.'

She watched as each of the men in the second line reloaded their muskets, guided by others. When all was ready, on a command they stepped forward and fired another volley into the embankment. They were ordered and disciplined, and she was ashamed for her question about Bolton Hall.

She thought back to Alfred Brenner leaning into the King's coach. 'My God', she whispered 'he could easily have carried a pistol, instead of a fistful of complaints. It seems the King's life now depends on the restraint of his subjects.'

Chapter 12

House of Commons

Tom waited impatiently on the steps of St. Stephen's Chapel for Barty Hopkins. Parliament was reconvening after the harvest recess and he had not seen his friend for well over a month. There had been no further attacks on the Tallants or their property but he was anxious to hear any news about Robert Petty's investigations.

The familiar bustling figure appeared, walking busily across Old Palace Yard in his direction. 'My dear Tom. Forgive my tardiness. The roads to Westminster are more choked than ever. Come, let us secure a seat.' They entered the familiar surroundings of the chapel, home to Parliament's House of Commons for almost a hundred years. Other members were crisscrossing the floor, their exchanged greetings echoing in the chamber as the two of them found space on the benches opposite where John Pym sat. The leader of the Puritan group was expected to provide the opening address.

'Robert tells me your family has not suffered any further attacks, thank God.'

'Yes. It's a relief but, without knowing who was responsible, it's difficult to relax. Has he discovered anything from his contacts?'

'I fear not but, as you know, Robert has the grip of a bulldog and won't let go until he has shaken something loose!' Barty laughed.

'And what of the murder investigation?'

His friend moved closer and whispered: 'Again, no news, but

I am glad of it. When two Jesuit priests are killed in identical manner and swift succession, we fear some mad soul has extermination in mind. But the murders have stopped as quickly as they begun. We have no idea why, but it's a great relief.'

'Maybe the killer himself came to grief, over another matter. You never know in the murky underworld these people inhabit.'

'I was rather hoping for divine intervention, but your suggestion is more likely and just as welcome. Just as long as the killing has stopped!'

The chamber was filling rapidly. All seats were now taken with late arrivals gathering at the back. 'Did you return to Banbury during the recess?' Tom asked, eyeing the growing crowd. 'How is the harvest?'

'Sufficiently plentiful, thank the Lord. Bread prices should remain stable.'

'Not so in Ireland apparently,' Tom answered. 'I hear the harvest has all but failed and there will be shortages. Not a good sign with winter approaching. I sense trouble over the water.'

'We have enough of that here,' Barty responded. 'I have spoken to other members from country boroughs. There's growing unease again that the Puritan reforms are going too far. They appeared to be momentarily checked by the adverse reaction to Strafford's execution, but Pym is whipping the horses again, driving his ambitions forward.'

Tom knew where his friend's sympathies lay and gave him a questioning look.

'No, really. It's true. The people of Banbury were glad to see the back of the King's Ship Money and the Star Chamber. Those needed to be put right. But it's emboldened the Puritans who are now challenging the vary fabric of the church, how people worship, the Prayer Book. They have embarked on a moral crusade and it's causing a lot of unrest.'

A voice arose above the hubbub. As the Speaker called the House to order, outlining the business of the day, he reflected on what Barty had said. Where would it stop, this conflict spreading from Banbury to Bolton Hall, afflicting all it touched with anger and discord.

Silence descended on the chapel as John Pym rose to speak. He was renowned for his detailed discourses, so the House was settling in for a lengthy listen. Pym outlined the list of grievances against the King that he wished to explain in more detail, when a member sitting behind tapped him on the shoulder and handed over a written message, whispering in his ear. Pym appeared annoyed by the interruption but broke the seal and unfolded the paper. He looked puzzled for several seconds, then suddenly recoiled, throwing the paper to the floor. As he did, Tom noticed a yellow and brown stained rag drop from inside the package, landing at Pym's feet stood.

'What infamy is this?' he shouted. 'Am I to be poisoned within the House itself? Is the voice of Parliament to be silenced in this foul, corrupted manner. 'Tis a plague rag!'

There was a moment of disbelief then panic consumed the chamber. As one, the members pushed back, as far away from Pym as possible. Word spread through the crowd who surged for the exit. The Serjeant at Arms drew his sword and hammered the pommel repeatedly on his bench to retain control, bawling 'order!' over and over again at the top of his voice.

'Is that what I think it is?' Tom shouted to Barty.

'Oh my goodness. It certainly appears to be a piece of winding sheet, from a poor unfortunate's body. But why does Pym think it's from a plague victim?'

'Presumably there was something in the message. It looks like you were right. People have had enough.'

Some sense of order began to return to the Commons as the

members gathered at the back of the room, many pressing handkerchiefs to their face. The discoloured rag remained on the Commons' floor, now surrounded by empty benches. John Pym could be seen remonstrating with the man who passed him the message, who was shrugging his shoulders and shaking his head.

'I would not like to be that man,' Tom continued, 'the unwitting deliverer of such a deadly message. No one would knowingly handle such a dangerous package. We need to go. Come, let's stand in line to leave the building. We will have to wait outside while they remove the offending item and sweeten the air.'

Barty didn't move. His face, so often a picture of merriment, was grey and stony, his eyes wide with shock. 'A barrow load of rosemary and lavender will no longer sweeten the air in this chamber, or anywhere in London for that matter. It's a plague that afflicts us all right, a plague of madness, and I fear for England's future, I truly do'.

Chapter 13

Bolton Hall

Tom picked up a handful of soil, rubbing it between thumb and fingers.

His father watched him enquiringly 'Any good?'

'Hmm. There's clay, but not too much. Probably drains quite well. Looks fertile. Yes, I'd be happy to grow plants in this.'

Ralph surveyed the field and Bolton Hall in the middle distance. Rays from the pale late morning sun caught a dusting of light frost on the hedgerow nearby, and the branches sparkled. A group of finches darted in and out of the hedge, fluttering their wings and chattering loudly. 'Thank you, Tom. You've given me plenty to think about.'

'You're considering buying this for mother?'

'Yes. When I was told this field next to us was available, it seemed too good to miss, with your mother's birthday approaching. We could extend the garden and she would have another project to keep her happy. One patch of earth looks like any other to me, so I needed your expertise.'

'Well, I'm sure she will be thrilled. Increasingly, merchants are returning from their travels with boxes of seed. It occupies little onboard space and there's a growing market here in London. She'll have plenty of new plants to raise.'

'Your mother often states she only married me because I can stock her garden with the wonders of the world,' his father grunted, but with a smile on his face.

A desperate scream shattered the calm. A woman's voice.

'What the devil!' Ralph exclaimed.

There was another, followed by an anguished cry of 'No, no!'

'It's coming from the house,' Tom shouted and they both leapt forward, sprinting towards Bolton Hall. They scrambled over the hard, rutted ground heading for a gate in the field's corner. There were more shouts and then a pistol shot, greeted by the caw-caw cry of the rooks deserting the treetops at Bolton Hall.

'Oh my God,' he cried and stumbled again on the rough soil. Would he ever reach the gate and the lane beyond to his parent's house? He could hear his father breathing hard behind him and then a yell of pain from the house - a man's voice this time, cursing and shouting.

At last, Tom reached the open gate and started to sprint up the track to Bolton Hall, pumping his legs. He could no longer hear his father as he surged ahead, towards the hedge at the rear of the Tallants' garden. His head was filled with the pounding of his heart and the sound of his increasingly laboured footsteps on the lane. His lungs were burning and his mind swimming as the panic rose in him.

'Stop there. Help is coming. Help is coming!' - the booming voice of his father who, unable to match Tom's speed, was making his presence felt from a distance.

He stumbled through the side gate into the rear of Bolton Hall. The garden was empty. Hands resting on his knees, he desperately gulped lungfuls of air. He tried to call his mother but couldn't make enough sound. Staggering back to the gate, he saw his father coming towards him, his progress now reduced to an unsteady jog. Tom turned left and continued up the path to the front corner of the Hall. Still there was no one but he could hear a woman sobbing. He continued to circuit the house, past the front door, before turning left at the far edge of the building. The sound was louder now and he followed the side of the house through the gate into the kitchen yard.

He slid to a halt. His mother was kneeling in the yard with her back to him, leaning over the body of the Dutch twin Jan, a folded cloth covered in blood pressed against his side. She glanced over her shoulder. 'Tom! Thank God. I need you to hold this, press it tightly against the wound while I get more cloths.'

If he hadn't known better, he would have put his mother's matter-of-fact manner down to shock. But he knew Beatrix Tallant was one of those singular people who remain calm, in fact become calmer, in any crisis.

Tom did as he was told while his mother ran into the kitchen. Jan was very still and pale, his breathing shallow. His father stumbled through the gate into the yard. 'Sweet Jesu,' he exclaimed, surveying the scene. 'Your mother, and Ellen, are they alright?'

'Mother seems unharmed,' Tom replied as he renewed the pressure on Jan's wound, the blood continuing to seep through the cloth.

'And so is Ellen, thanks to Jan.' It was his mother, returning with fresh cloths to stem the bleeding. 'Ralph, she is in the drawing room, very shaken. Please go to her. Tom I will take over here. You must fetch Elizabeth. I need her nursing skills. Go now. Quick!'

'I will send a servant to her house immediately. I must find who did this before they make their escape,' and wearily picking himself up, he sprinted towards the entrance, returning several minutes later.

'There's no sign but I can see dust in the air on the road entering Clerkenwell. If that's them, I'll never catch them on Meg before they're inside the City wall.'

Two hours later, Ralph, Beatrix and Tom were sitting in the drawing room at Bolton Hall, piecing together what happened.

'So you are in no doubt that their aim was to kidnap Ellen?'

Beatrix frowned at her husband's question. 'No doubt? You ask a lot, given the utter confusion and terror. But, yes, that seemed to be the reason for their visit. Five of them came to the house while I was in the back garden and Ellen was inside. One, a woman, knocked at the door while the other four hid in the bushes. She had a message for Ellen and was dressed and acted respectfully. The servant asked her to wait outside but when he went to close the door, the other four appeared and pushed their way in.

'They rounded everyone up, including me, in the kitchen yard, holding a knife to the servant's throat to persuade us to cooperate. But they didn't know Mark was in the stables, doing a job for me, and Jan was helping him. And neither of them had a clue what was happening.

'One of the men grabbed Ellen to separate her from the others. She screamed and that's when the trouble started.'

'That will be the scream we heard,' Tom said.

'And so did Jan and Mark', his mother continued. 'Moments later Mark arrived in the kitchen yard, followed by Jan carrying his flintlock pistol, and all hell broke loose.'

'Jan had a pistol? Was it loaded?' he asked.

'Yes. I told him to keep it close at all times, given the situation. He must have had it with him in the stables.' Ralph answered.

'Jan's English is not so good, so he pointed the pistol at the tallest man, saying 'Lady Ellen, let go' over and over. One of the gang must have thought the gun was not loaded and rushed Jan, who shot him in the leg. The man went down clutching his thigh and swearing, while the other three threw themselves at Mark and Jan, and the woman kept hold of Ellen. Mark seemed eager for the fight, probably after the punishment he received last time, and he started wrestling with one of them while the other two went for Jan.'

'They stood either side of him to divide his attention. Jan ran at the tallest who pulled a knife. He was so brave. He didn't hesitate for a moment, continuing his charge and knocking the man to the ground, then punching him in the face over and over.

'The other man dragged Ellen to the gate, helped by the woman. Jan grabbed him and he let go of Ellen, kicking Jan hard. Meanwhile Mark had felled one and turned his attention to the tall man who had been punched by Jan.

'We were getting the upper hand and then…and then everything became a disaster. Sensing they were in trouble, the woman let go of Ellen and calmly took a dagger from her belt and stabbed Jan in the side, twice and he collapsed to the floor. Everyone stopped, then we heard Ralph's voice, saying you were coming. It seemed to stir Ellen who, free of the woman's grip, ran back to the kitchen shouting 'My father is coming, he's coming. Now you will suffer.'

At that, the man and woman nodded to each other and ran towards Mark, threatening him with the knife. He backed off and the gang picked up their injured friend, escaped through the gate and ran away from the house.

A minute later you arrived while I was trying to stop Jan's bleeding.

'How is he?'

He's in his bedroom, tended by Elizabeth. His wounds are deep and I fear for him.'

Beatrix gazed around the yard, a beleaguered expression on her face: 'We must all pray for Jan. I owe my daughter's safety and possibly her life to that brave young man.'

Chapter 14

Little Salisbury House

Lucy Carlisle clapped her hands like an excited child and broke into a beaming smile.

'My goodness. How clever you are, Elizabeth. You have quite made my day.'

They were sitting in the elegant drawing room at Little Salisbury House. Elizabeth had arrived to find the Countess of Carlisle in consultation with her dressmaker, fabric swatches and patterns scattered across the floor. The man was promptly dismissed, and Lucy waited until he had hurriedly gathered his samples and left before retrieving a letter from her writing desk.

'This message is from a good friend in the intelligence service. He prides himself as a code-breaker and with good reason. He has cracked many in his time for kings and queens across Europe. I thought 'what better way to test yours', so I sent him a sample.' Lucy picked up the letter again, 'which he describes it as 'unfathomable' and begs me to tell him who created it!'

Elizabeth lent forward. 'But Lady Carlisle, you promised...'

'Do not worry, my dear. Now I have such an important friend, the last thought in my mind is to share you! Your obvious genius for coding is safe with me. But you must tell. How did you think it up?'

'Like all my codes, it's based on new thinking in mathematical science. In my experience, it's an area of singular ignorance among most courtiers and even their intelligencers, so it suits my purpose. This latest cipher is based on logarithms.'

'Logar...?' Lucy struggled with the word but appeared impressed.

'I find code breakers can be daunted by a purely numerical code, so the cipher I have created for you requires not one, but two sets of numbers.

'Most frustrating.'

'Hopefully. Let me explain. You have a message you want to send. First, you use a coding book to assign a number for each letter in the message. For example the letter 'A' could be the number '8'. As you know, many ciphers use this method. All the letters are transformed into a set of numbers which, on the face of it, cannot be deciphered. But if someone steals your coding book, it is a simple matter to look up each number and find the corresponding letter. Soon the message is revealed'.

'As I have discovered in the past, to my cost,' Lucy smiled ruefully.

'But now I have added a second set of numbers, using a specific logarithm table based on the number 2. So, as we said, let's imagine the letter A is represented by the number 8 in your code book. Using your logarithms, it would then change from 8 to the number 3.

'Why?' Lucy asked, her brow now creased with a frown.

'Because logarithms tell you how many of one number you need to make another number. In this case, you require three number 2s to make 8 – 2 times 2 is 4, and 2 times 4 makes 8. So the new code number for 8 is 3!

'Elizabeth. You are doing a marvellous job so far explaining your system to a dunce like me. I am keeping pace, just. Pray continue, but not too expeditiously.'

So, if you base all your logarithm calculations on the number 2, you can produce a second number for every letter in the alphabet. So 'A' becomes 8 , which becomes 3. And, say the letter 'B' is 32 in your code book. You look at your logarithm table and you find the number 2 is used 5 times to make 32. So the new number for B changes from 32 to ...

'5?'

'Yes! It's that simple to use, and with this double lock, your secrets are safe even if your coding book is stolen. Equally if, by unlikely chance, your enemy realised your cipher was based on logarithms, they would still require the code book to make sense of it.

'There is no such thing as a foolproof code. So my aim, with each new cipher, is to stretch the probabilities of discovery still further. This should give you the security you require.

'Who is the genius who thought of log...logarithms ? I must write to him with my congratulations.'

'They were developed by a Scottish mathematician John Napier. Sadly he has since died. But others continue his work, such as John Pell whose 'Introduction to Mathematics' has taught me much. I am in occasional correspondence with him.'

Lucy sat back and regarded Elizabeth anew. 'Is it commonplace for you to correspond with men of learning?'

'Oh yes. On many matters of natural science and mathematics. There are so many discoveries...almost every week.'

'That cannot be easy. A woman on her own. Are you not mocked by men and your intelligence insulted?'

She smiled and lowered her eyes. 'Indeed, I have lost count of how often I am told to 'know my place', but rarely by scientists; and the views of others are not really important, are they?'

Lucy broke into spontaneous applause 'Elizabeth Seymour. I like your spirit! I think you and I will have much to talk about in the future. But in truth, I am also a little jealous of your learning. Did your father encourage your education?'

'Yes. I am fortunate that both my parents supported my

interest in mathematics and science. Now I have grown up, I can see what an unusual approach that was, and am grateful for it.'

'Unusual? I would say unique. My father, the Earl of Northumberland, had a natural curiosity and he valued knowledge. He too was interested in science and spent much of his time conducting experiments while imprisoned in the Tower of London.'

'Yes, I have heard of him -the 'Wizard Earl?'.

Lucy frowned at her father's nickname. 'My brother Algernon was tutored daily by scholars and scientists, but father had no interest whatsoever in educating either Dorothy, my elder sister, or me. When we visited him in the Tower, he used to say 'women are as wise at 15 as at 50'.

Elizabeth's face became animated. 'You used to visit him in the Tower? Then did you meet Thomas Harriot? I believe he was the first person to make a drawing of the Moon through a telescope, even before Galileo! Your father was his patron. He was known as one of the Earl's Magi.'

Lucy paused and then went again to her writing desk, returning with another piece of paper. She sat at the table and handed it to Elizabeth. 'This is a letter to Dorothy that I have started. Read it. No, please do, there is nothing scandalous in it - yet.'

She took the letter and started to read its contents. She stopped at the second line, lowered the page and her eyes.

'What do you see?'

Elizabeth looked up and held Lucy's gaze. She spoke softly. 'I see you have not had the opportunity so far in your life to express yourself clearly.'

'Nicely put. Honest yet careful. I see we *are* going to get on famously, young lady. Yes, I cannot spell. So you can see that my father's world of wizardry and magi was denied me, and my sister, as was any sort of useful education. I have no idea who Thomas Harriot was, or is. When I send hand-written invitations to the lords of the land to attend my salons, they never comment on my spelling. Maybe they expect little better from a woman, or perhaps they are too busy staring at my bosom. Either way, it says naught for their appreciation of my intellect, does it?'

Elizabeth was finding it difficult to divine Lucy's mood or feelings, which was not a common experience for her. Increasingly, she was fascinated by this woman.

'When my husband, the Earl of Carlisle, was alive our parties were the talk of London. We entertained lavishly and, in time, I became the darling of the Royal Court. This allowed my husband to promote his influence over the King in affairs of state. I also was taken increasingly into the Queen's confidence. When my husband died, I had to find other ways to sustain that influence.'

'Why?'

'Why? Well, why not? Despite my lack of education, I had risen to a position of importance. I *knew* this was not simply because of my husband and I was determined to prove that. I would use every natural asset I possessed – yes, in particular my attractiveness to men - to retain my position at court as the Queen's trusted and influential advisor.'

'That could not have been easy.'

'Certainly not. I had to smile and compliment men who turned my stomach. Endure dreadful creatures like Sir John Suckling sullying my reputation – Suckling Pig I call him – trampled underfoot by his vile poetry about me, suggesting I was a common courtesan, making my way on my back.'

'Then I met Thomas, the Earl of Strafford. Again the court tittle-tattlers said he was my lover. They couldn't imagine that we might like each other but no more. He respected me, admired my independence. But in the end even he let me down. I trusted his advice on my Irish investments, but now it's becoming clear he may have profited from some of the dealings undertaken on my behalf.'

'So you see Elizabeth, you'll find the life of an independent woman, both in thought and deed, is not easy. But still worth the trouble, I think.'

Chapter 15

Waterman's Lane, Alsatia

The boy collapsed to the floor, felled by a lacerating blow to his face. Billy Boy kicked him hard in the ribs and then stood astride his victim, looking at Jack Dancer, his eyes shining in triumph.

'Nicely done Billy, but I'd remove those brass knucks if you want to leave him with any face.'

Billy grinned as he examined the blood smearing a crude metal band covering his right fist. 'Aw, that's a shame Jack. I was starting to enjoy myself. He's no good for us. There's no brag about him.'

Each day, crowds of street urchins pursued Dancer, begging to join his gang of cutpurses, card sharps and conmen. His rule of admission was simple. If they could handle themselves against Billy, they got a month's trial. The deciding fight was held in a disused warehouse in Waterman's Lane, deep in the heart of Alsatia. It was one of several Dancer owned in the haven. He liked to keep on the move, and this warehouse was just yards from the Whitefriars' Stairs onto the river, should he need a quick exit.

'So, he's failed the Billy Boy test, has he?'

'That he has, a chit of a boy, I've gone gentle with....aaargh!'

Billy roared with pain as the boy beneath him suddenly punched upwards, powering his fist into Billy's crutch with a straight right arm. He fell forwards in a heap, clutching his groin. Dancer erupted into a rasping laugh, shaking his head.

The boy slowly pushed Billy off him and staggered to his feet.

He stood in front of Dancer, the right side of his face ripped and bleeding.

'Well, you're a cunning shaver, aren't you boy? Got balls too, I'll give you that. Can't say the same for Billy any more. What's yer name again?'

'Job, sir', the boy gasped, swaying unsteadily.

'Job? The righteous man persecuted by Satan? Well if you join us Job, you'll see that's true enough.' Job gave Jack a puzzled look, his swollen right eye starting to close. Billy was now resting on his haunches, vomiting on the yard floor.

'You have no idea what I'm talking about, do you? Step out of line and you'll soon find out. Anyhow, you'll do for us. You've got guts but we'll have to teach you how to fight proper. Billy will do that. He'll enjoy it.' A smile flickered across Job's face before his eyes turned into the top of his head and he fell in a heap.

Dancer surveyed the yard, Billy now on his back and Job collapsed next to him. He shook his head, stood and walked to a trough, returning with a wooden pail of dirty water, which he threw in Billy's face. 'You're becoming too cocky, Billy. Left yourself wide open there. C'mon, stand up. We need to talk'.

Still retching, Billy Boy hobbled towards Dancer. 'That whoreson. I'll enjoy showing him the ropes.'

'As you should Billy, but keep your knucks in your pocket, you hear? It's not the boy's fault you gave him an easy target. His name's Job, by the way. So, back to business. I've got some good news for you. You can stop looking for Jesuit priests, not that you were any good at it.'

Billy Boy scowled. 'They've all gone to ground or left the country. All this shit about papist plots. There aren't any of them left.'

Dancer whipped out his left arm and slapped Billy on the side of his head. 'Don't get arsey with me, Billy Boy. Not after that limp-dick performance. You write off the Catholic Church at your peril. They're here all right. Biding their time.

'This job isn't just about knifing the religious sort, much as I enjoy that. We've been searching for a very rare pearl who can unlock untold riches. But there's more ways to kill a dog than hanging, Billy Boy, so we're changing our tactics. The search moves on from the Jesuits to something else. And I know where. We need to get a move on, so I will go and take a look-see and then we'll plan our move. Get the boys prepared.'

Chapter 16

The Royal Exchange, Cornhill

Tom looked up at the familiar sight of the gilded grasshopper weather vane as he approached the Royal Exchange. Normally it raised a smile but his business today in London's trading centre weighed heavily on him. He was meeting Barty and Robert Petty and was desperate to make progress in the hunt for the attackers of Bolton Hall.

He pushed his way through the rag-tag band of street sellers who regularly crowded around the building's southern entrance on Cornhill. Lemons and oranges were pressed into his hands by women, some half-drunk, desperate to make some coin. A man was trying to persuade another merchant to buy his dog, a thin mangy creature held on a short piece of twine, and promised him the 'best ratter in London'. He could feel their frantic hopelessness and thought of the woman in the warehouse attempting to claim Josh Wilding's wages.

He entered the building and kept his head down. He wanted this meeting to be private. The Tallants sold most of their spices at the Exchange and the building manager had given him the use of an empty first floor shop as a favour. But he needed to get there without being seen. He had to cross a corner of the busy trading floor to reach the stairs, and was wondering how to achieve this unnoticed when a commotion broke out behind him.

He could hear discordant music and shouting coming from the street. He darted behind a pillar as everyone in the Exchange turned to look at the Cornhill entrance. This was not what he needed. The street hawkers had been joined by another group including, on its hind legs, a large brown bear. Tom blinked and saw the beast was being led on a thick rope by a bear ward. A monkey was balanced on its right shoulder, with three minstrels following, dressed in ragged harlequin costumes, playing fiddle jigs tunelessly.

This time he did allow himself a smile. The local bear-bating pit must have a show tonight, and their timing was perfect. Their attempt to attract customers was meeting with mixed success, with some merchants complaining loudly about disruption to their business. A scuffle broke out and he slipped away unseen to the stairwell.

His friends were waiting in a private back room of the empty shop.

'What fun and games!' Barty said, excitedly. 'Was that really a bear in the Exchange? We couldn't see from the balcony. Whatever next!'

'Yes, the bear ward is drumming up business for tonight's fight.'

''Tis a cruel entertainment, and no type of sport', Petty said.

'Well, of course, absolutely' Barty mumbled , as they all sat down. 'So, let's get to business and compare notes on our investigation. By Jesu's name,

what a state of affairs! Your parents' home is first ransacked and then attacked by a wicked gang trying to kidnap Ellen,' he exclaimed. 'How is your dear sister?'

'Initially she was very shaken and would not leave the house,' Tom replied. 'However she is now regaining her confidence. Ellen is tougher than she looks. She takes after our mother.'

'I'm glad to hear it. Do you think these two outrageous incidents are connected?'

He was surprised by Barty's question. 'If we lived in the City I would say possibly not, as there is so much disorder on the streets. But out beyond Clerkenwell? In the countryside? I feel they surely must be linked. Bolton Hall is not a place you stumble upon by chance.'

Robert Petty nodded his agreement, 'I agree, it's too much of a coincidence. It's clear in my mind the same wretches were behind both attacks. And I'm pleased to say I may finally have made progress in tracking down who is responsible.'

'You know who did it?'

Petty's brow furrowed as he put his palms forward in a pacifying gesture.

'Let us not get ahead of ourselves. As you know, I am working my contacts hard in the City. I picked up plenty of rumours and accusations, but the mood on the streets currently is so poisonous it's taken a long time to sort the wheat from the chaff. Under closer scrutiny, almost all the suggestions proved to be malicious, designed to discredit individuals. However I have found one that could be more promising.'

'Please Robert. Do not hold me in suspense. This is the first good news I have received in this whole dreadful affair. Do we have a name?'

'Not yet and I must impress upon you I'm at the early stages of my investigation. It may, once again, only be spiteful gossip.'

'Investigation?' Barty commented. 'You called it an investigation? Does that infer your private research on Tom's behalf may soon become the formal business of the Merchant Adventurers, and it is another merchant who is responsible?'

His eyes were alight with a sharp intelligence that belied his innocent appearance. Petty had made a slip and he was on it in a flash.

Petty grimaced at his own error. 'It's too early to say. I must stress the importance of not spreading this information further. It is only a suggestion, but it has come from two different and reliable sources. However it all may come to nothing. My role as an investigator for the Merchant Adventurers would be in jeopardy if I besmirched the reputation of one of its members, without gathering compelling evidence first.'

'But you do know who it is? A member of the Adventurers?' Tom continued.

'No! 'Petty exclaimed with exasperation. 'I have no names at present.'

Barty clasped Tom's forearm. 'I share your desire to find those responsible but we must let Robert proceed with due caution. It will bring results, I can assure you, if there is any truth in the claim.'

The three sat in silence for several minutes and then Petty continued, speaking quietly. 'I have learned that someone harbours jealousy over the Tallants' success in the spice trade. That person feels your family has acquired a source of trading information that's been very much to your advantage in recent years. This gives you access to new supplies of high quality spices in the Indies, at prices that undercut your rivals.'

Tom's shoulders sagged with disappointment. 'Robert, I thank you for your efforts but there is nothing new in this. Yes, we do regularly acquire superior quality spices but this is due to our excellent agents in India and beyond. Our rivals frequently grumble about it, but nothing has changed to make one of them suddenly resort to kidnapping my sister!'

'You have told me this before.' Petty acknowledged. 'But this accusation goes further. It's said you are trading information with our great rivals the Dutch East India Company, using their knowledge to gain this advantage. And the question is 'what do you give them in return?'

Barty coughed and lent forward to Petty, almost whispering. 'Let us be clear, Robert. When you say investigation, who is now under scrutiny - the perpetrator of these terrible crimes at Bolton Hall, or the Tallant family themselves?'

Robert Petty stared at Tom with his deep brown unblinking

eyes.

'I have to say, at the moment, nothing can be ruled out. So, I'm sorry, but it has to be both.'

Chapter 17

Bolton Hall

Ralph Tallant gave his son a disbelieving look.

'You're telling me the person behind the attacks could be a fellow City merchant? I'm sorry, but I don't believe it.'

They were sitting in the drawing room at Bolton Hall. Outside the wind was howling, blowing squally showers almost horizontally across the garden. Tom was appreciating the heat from the wood fire crackling in the fireplace. Beatrix Tallant and Elizabeth were attending to Jan upstairs. His condition had not improved since the attack, despite their care and frequent visits from his brother, and he flitted in and out of consciousness. Yesterday he had started a fever and both were worried an infection had developed.

'I don't want to believe it either father, and Petty stresses he has much work still to do. But after weeks of investigation, it's the only possibility he's taking seriously.

'That does not make it true. The very idea is absurd.'

Tom sighed in exasperation. 'You, yourself, have warned me that the City can be a snake pit, with its own rules, and there is anti-Dutch sentiment among some merchants. You must agree, Petty's suggestion is not entirely fanciful.'

'It's one thing for a merchant to bear a grudge against the Dutch and make malicious gossip to damage their reputation. Quite another to raid our house and attempt to kidnap your sister!'

Ralph leaned forward and picked up a small log from the wood basket next to him. 'You're right, the City does have its own rules, but it would be unthinkable for a rival merchant to launch such a visible assault on our family. It's far too public. Attracts too much attention,' and at this he threw the log into the grate sending a shower of sparks into the air. 'No, if a merchant was responsible, the deed would be done with a stiletto between the ribs…*silenziosamente*…silently. Believe me.'

'So you don't dismiss the possibility, just the method?'

Ralph's face coloured. 'Tom that's enough! We have sufficient concerns to occupy our minds without this foolish notion of Petty's. I've said before, this mob violence is more likely the work of John Pym or another of his Puritan gang. You can now see it everyday throughout the City, and its getting worse.'

'Yes, but not so far outside the City walls, surely?'

'There's trouble erupting throughout the counties! Only this week I've been told of popish plots in Guildford and Norwich. Pym has got the hot-gospellors stirring up mischief all over the country, causing panic.'

'That's true. I know of fights in Essex between Puritans and those who do not wish to see changes to their church.'

'Exactly. Pym's taking his battle beyond the streets of London, and where better than the homes of merchants which are still close enough to be reached by his gang of Apprentice Boys?'

'But why us?'

'Why not? In the eyes of the mob, merchants have wealth and power and all support the King even though, as we know, quite a number are reformers. You must understand, as we have seen before, that it doesn't matter what is true, just what people believe to be true. They don't want proof and, if any did, they would just point to your refusal to sign Strafford's death warrant.'

Their conversation paused and Tom could faintly hear his mother upstairs calling to the maid, a note of urgency in her voice. Ralph reached over and gripped his forearm. 'Tom, we have no choice. We must fight fire with fire. Which is why I have already acted against Pym and his junto.'

He was shocked by the quiet ferocity in his father's voice. 'What do you mean?'

Ralph paused. He was weighing his next words carefully.

'What I am about to tell you must never be repeated outside this room. Do you understand?' He nodded. What had his father done?

'Do you recall in Parliament, when John Pym received a letter containing a piece of binding from a plague victim?'

He thought back to the shock of that moment, the suspension of the session and, with it, Pym's speech. 'I'm hardly likely to forget it, as I was so close to Pym.'

Ralph smiled. 'You were perfectly safe. You could have blown your nose on that rag without any ill effect.'

He gaped at his father, momentarily lost for words. 'What do you mean? How could you know that?'

'Because I sent that message. I used one of my old contacts in the Commons. He couldn't have timed it better, handing it to Pym as he was launching into one of his interminable speeches and had the attention of the whole House.'

'And the cloth?'

'An old rag I found in the kitchen here at Bolton, used to wrap a leg of mutton, I believe, so it was suitably stained. I included a message – no name, of course – a piece of nonsense making it clear to Pym he was holding a plague rag, and more would follow if he didn't back off, but with no other specifics.'

'But, what a risk! If you'd been discovered, you'd now be in the Tower, your reputation – and our business –ruined.'

'Yes, a risk, but a calculated one. There was nothing in the message to identify me and my contact was a trusted old friend who shared my views on Pym. He knew the rag was safe and he had his story ready. If asked, the sealed letter was given to him by a stranger outside the chamber who requested it be handed to Pym immediately.

'I sent the rag as a reprisal – warning Pym off. If there was then another attack on Bolton Hall, I'd know he was my man. And, of course, that's what happened. The members of the Puritan junto are so arrogant. If you are not with them, you are against them and attacking any opposition is God's will.

'So you were anticipating another attempt on our house?

'Yes, but not so soon, or so savage.' Tom's father stared at the floor, his hands clenched tight together.

'But Ellen and Jan?'

Ralph nodded. 'I had no idea Pym would go to such lengths. I miscalculated, and now I live with the consequences. Thank God Ellen is safe, but Jan…'

He pondered his father's story. It had blown Petty's theory of a rival merchant out of his mind. He had witnessed the determination of the junto previously in the Commons and their inflamed language about papist plots. And his father was right about their insufferable certainty. The account seemed real and credible. He would have to talk again with Petty and Barty.

There was a knock on the door and his mother entered, followed by Elizabeth. Both looked exhausted. As they approached, he could see their faces, wet with tears.

'He's gone. Jan has gone.' Beatrix whispered. 'That brave boy has finally succumbed. He has given his life to save Ellen.'

He walked to Elizabeth and took her hand. 'Was it the fever?'

'Yes. An infection had taken hold and he was already very

weak from losing so much blood. I'm so sorry, Sir Ralph, but I couldn't save him.'

She buried her face in Tom's chest and submitted to a wave of wracking sobs that shook her body. Still holding her, he looked at his father, rooted to the spot, his face ashen and haggard.

'Damn, damn, damn,' Ralph murmured. 'I shall write to Jonas at once and then I must tell Dirck.'

Chapter 18

The Tallant warehouse

Tom lay in his bed at the warehouse, listening in the dark to the creaking of a ship's rigging in the breeze.

He stared at the ceiling, his mind full of images from the previous day: Dirck sitting on Jan's bed hugging his brother's lifeless form, whispering to him desperately in Dutch as he rocked back and forth; Ellen's grief when she was given the news, and his mother repeatedly saying it was not her fault; and above all, his father's stony expression of shock and guilt.

Dirck was eventually persuaded to return to the warehouse, where he sat on the wharf looking at the river, his only company a rapidly emptying bottle of brandy. He finally went to his bed and managed to sleep but, three hours later, Tom was still awake.

What of his father? Would his conscience be troubled enough to deny him sleep? Pym's immediate retaliation to the plague letter made it plain who was behind the attacks on Bolton Hall, but at what cost? Uncle Jonas would be furious. The parents of the twins were close friends in Amsterdam and the boys had been entrusted to his care. When agreeing to Ralph's request for extra bodies, he would have relied on his brother not to place them in extreme danger. Jan's death was a disaster for the Tallants.

He turned over in his bed and attempted once again to empty his mind. He concentrated on the occasional noise from the rigging, nothing else. It reminded him of sleeping on board ship, without the swell of the waves. Eventually, his thoughts settled and the creaking merged with other sounds in the wooden building – the slight movement of old joists, the scrabble of a mouse looking for grain and the occasional rattle of a loose shutter disturbed by the breeze.

What was that knocking, coming from below? He was alert again and totally focused on something new he could define. He sat up in bed, stock still. Ten, fifteen seconds passed…and there it was again, and then again.

His bedroom was on the first floor of the warehouse, overlooking the river and the wharf below. He stood and crept towards its window, stopping every couple of steps, his ears straining. He reached the window and checked the wharf. The moon was partly behind a small bank of cloud, giving enough light to see the familiar contours of the dock and the ship moored against it, but little else. Was that a movement, by the deck of the ship? He stared hard but saw nothing.

Again there was knocking, quieter this time. He attempted to place it within the inky blackness, but it was hopeless. Picking up his sword, Tom tiptoed down the warehouse stairs, stopping regularly to listen, but there was nothing. He was cold and regretting leaving his bed and, on reaching the ground floor, strode to the back door with less caution.

Removing the sword from its scabbard, he carefully undid a bolt, opened the door and stepped into the dark outside. The cloud had thickened in front of the moon and a cool breeze touched his face as he waited for his eyes to adjust.

There was another knock, much clearer now, further down the wharf, next to the ship's side. He advanced slowly, sword drawn. The vessel docked yesterday and its cargo had been unloaded. Hatches and doors secured, it would sail to Rotherhithe for repairs in the morning. If it was looters he'd disturbed, they'd be out of luck; but so would he, as no help would be at hand. As he inched forward, a dark shape started to form in the black void in front of him. He held his breath and took one more step. He was in touching distance. Now or never.

Tom called out. 'Stand firm there. I have you covered by my sword.' The words echoed across the wharf. Nothing. The shape didn't move and all remained calm. Exasperated, he took another step and prodded the shape with his blade. It was a barrel resting against the ship, the rise and fall of its hull occasionally knocking the side of the keg.

He could feel himself flush. He hoped Isaac, sleeping in his room near the kitchen, hadn't heard him challenging a cooper's barrel. He would never live it down. With a rueful smile, he relaxed his shoulders, sheathed his sword and collapsed to the floor, felled by a single blow to the back of his head.

* * *

Ralph Tallant examined his son. 'That's a nasty blow. Expertly delivered to knock you out. You'll have a headache for a day or two.'

Tom was in his warehouse bed. He sat up and winced as he gingerly explored a large swelling behind his right ear. 'I suppose I am lucky it isn't worse.'

Ralph nodded. 'Whoever dealt with you then entered the warehouse through the back door and started rummaging around. They made enough noise to wake Dirck, even from his drunken stupor. He found three of them on their way up to the pepper store. By the time Isaac arrived with his halberd, one had a bloody nose and another was limping badly. One look at Isaac and the three of them took flight like jack rabbits.'

'How is Dirck?'

'Sore fists, so he's probably feeling better for hitting back at his brother's killers.'

'You think they're the same people who raided Bolton Hall, a gang of Pym's Apprentice Boy toughs?'

'Well unless we have suddenly become the pariahs of

London's merchant community, I don't think there can be any other explanation, do you?'

He sensed his father was more like his old self. He seemed to welcome the attack on the warehouse for the certainty it gave him about his enemy. That made Tom uneasy.

Chapter 19

The House of Lords

The Archbishop of York pulled up his fine lace sleeves and flexed his fists. He surveyed the baying crowd. What was it he felt? Fear? No. Something closer to contempt.

Minutes earlier, his carriage had entered the Old Palace Yard. From his raised vantage point, he could observe a sea of closely cropped heads ahead.. The Apprentice Boys were out in force, blocking his path to the House of Lords.

He half expected this. The bishops' support for the King in the Lords was proving troublesome to Pym and the Puritan junto. But if the bishops could not take their seats in the Lords, they could not vote. So the Apprentice Boys had been unleashed.

He frowned at the barefaced arrogance of Pym's stratagem. 'Well, it won't succeed, if I have anything to do with it' he murmured and urged his driver to move forward towards the House. The archbishop removed his Canterbury cap and pushed himself as far back into his seat as he could. No point in inviting trouble.

The Apprentice Boys were massing at the far end of the Yard looking towards the House of Lords, and their chant of 'No Bishops, No Popish Lords' grew louder as the archbishop edged closer towards them. Just when he thought that, perhaps, he might remain undetected, the cry went up. 'A bishop! Do we have a bishop?' A group had broken away and was running towards him. Thank God he'd had the sense to leave his official coach, complete with insignia, at home. He banged on the roof.

'Keep moving forward. Whatever you do, you must not stop' he shouted to his coachman. Within seconds the carriage was surrounded, swaying on its springs as the crowd jostled and pushed. The archbishop cautiously peered through the window and the first seeds of doubt were planted in his mind. The faces staring at him were contorted with rage. He had expected drunkenness, not fury.

His horses were still pushing their way through the throng with the Lords now almost within reach, but their progress was slowing. Hands clawed at the doors, trying to open them. The coachman's urged the horses forward. Why had he been allowed to stay on the carriage? With a chill, the archbishop realised the apprentices weren't interested in the driver, just his passenger.

A burly hand came through the right-side window, reaching for the door handle. The archbishop lashed out with his foot, stamping on the fingers of a large man, who disappeared into the melee, crying out in pain. He heard a grunting noise to his left and swiveled in his seat to see a boy half through the window, scrabbling to grab his surplice. He hit him hard in the face with his fist and pitched him back into the crowd. This gave the Apprentice Boys their first sight of his cassock and a roar went up. 'Tis a bishop! We have one!' The archbishop felt the cold sweat of fear running down his back. This was not protest. It was a lynch mob.

By now the coach had been forced to a halt. People at the rear scrabbled like rats to climb on to the roof. He realised that, unless he risked all, this coach could soon become his coffin. He fought a strong impulse to remain within its protection and hide away. He must get out, try to re-assert order and hail rescuers, if possible.

He took a deep breath and pushed at the door on his left. First the crush was too great but it eased as people saw what he was trying to do. They pulled back, momentarily quietened by his actions. 'Look at me,' he shouted, standing in the doorway. 'I am John Williams, once Bishop of Lincoln and a friend to you all.' The crowd were listening. 'I spoke out against Archbishop Laud's attempt to change your church worship. You cheered me then. I was locked in the Tower and church bells in London were pealed on my release. Why do you persecute me now?'

'Because you've taken the King's shilling again,' a voice cried out, 'so he'd make you Archbishop of York. That makes you worse than simply a bishop. You're a traitor too.' A roar went up. Williams was stunned. He'd started his new position less than a month ago and was relying on the mob not yet knowing he'd joined the King's side. This was something much more than the usual drunken Apprentice Boy melee. Someone had knowledge.

The crowd pushed forward, scenting blood. Williams tried to step back into the carriage but the protestors wouldn't let go of the door. Just as he feared the worst, he noticed Lord Dover pushing though the crush on his horse, followed by more mounted men. 'Make way! Make way!' they shouted as they used their powerful mounts to force the apprentices apart.

'Dover! Thank the Lord you have come!' he shouted. The protestors backed off and the archbishop could see he was no more than 30 yards from the entrance to the Lords. His new escort signaled him to get into his carriage that was now surrounded by horsemen.

John Williams slumped back in his seat and his coach started inching forward. Dazed, he looked at the vestment he always wore to the Lords. The fine lace was ripped and spattered with the blood of his young assailant. He examined his right hand, which was bruised and shaking. His contempt for the mob had gone, replaced by cold dread.

Chapter 20

The Manor House, Clerkenwell

Tom surveyed the night sky, studded with twinkling points of light, clear, but not cold for December. Perfect conditions for stargazing. Elizabeth sat next to him, humming contentedly as she adjusted her Kepler telescope, plumes of tobacco smoke rising from the clay pipe clenched between her teeth.

His mind went back to their first encounter in her parents' garden. The two of them, another starry night, and Ellen scandalised Elizabeth was meeting him unaccompanied. They talked about her love of life, the wonders of nature, and her hunger for discovery. He was captivated, and had remained so ever since.

They had returned to the same bench, at Elizabeth's request. She could see he was both troubled and conflicted and had suggested a search for the moons of Venus might be an effective remedy. He reached over and held her hand. She turned away from the telescope's eyepiece and moved nearer to him on the bench. The familiar smell of rose and lavender filled the night air as she reached over and kissed him gently on the cheek.

'It's a troubling time,' she said. 'I thought we might both benefit from the presence of the firmament, to soothe our minds and gain perspective.'

Two days ago, Jan's body had been shipped back to Amsterdam for burial. Dirck insisted he should remain in London to protect the Tallant family, but his pain at this final separation from his brother was a harrowing moment, the latest of many. Tom gazed at a single point in the sky. He experienced the familiar sensation of seeing more stars the longer he looked, only to watch them recede again into the black expanse - the closest he ever felt to God, to eternity.

'Thank you. Yes, it helps,' Tom replied. 'So. Let us think of other things. How are your navigational enquiries for my father progressing?'

'Slowly, but it is fascinating. It has led me down several rabbit holes of investigation. I am learning a great deal. Your mother has helped me to understand the work of Joan Bleau, a leading Dutch mapmaker who I have discovered. His latest portolan chart is well ahead of the field and could prove useful if we ever get to sea trials. Lady Beatrix has been very generous with her time, translating his Bleau's papers. I couldn't have managed without her. Although...'

He could hear the note of worry in Elizabeth's voice. 'What's the matter?'

'I am not sure but recently she seems less inclined to assist, as if she's preoccupied. But this is nonsense. Of course she's distracted by what has happened to poor Jan and Ellen. On occasions, I get too engrossed in my learning. I feel ashamed for even thinking about it, given what your mother has endured of late.'

Tom gave her arm a reassuring squeeze. 'Don't worry. I'm glad you have something else to occupy your mind. Presently I can only consider one thing.'

'The attacks?'

'Yes, I am trying to clear my mind and make sense of all that is happening. Robert is a very thorough investigator. He would not suspect a rival merchant if he didn't have firm suspicions. But talking to my father, it seems the assaults are definitely the work of Pym and his Puritan junto.'

'Can you be sure of that? I too have had some persistent

questions that refuse to be answered. Why would the Puritans attack the Tallants three times, twice at Bolton Hall and then the warehouse? Why single out your family? I couldn't make sense of it, so I sought the advice…of a friend.'

He noticed Elizabeth's hesitation. 'Not Nicholas Culpeper?'

'Yes. But Tom, hear me out.'

He bristled. Nicholas Culpeper was a topic of conversation they had learned to avoid. 'You didn't tell him about the attacks, did you?'

'He knew about them, at least the two at Bolton Hall. Incidents like that, in broad daylight, can't be hidden. Nicholas had heard nothing about Puritans choosing the Tallants as a target, and he feels such attacks would be out of character for Pym. Nick knows Pym is no angel and that he freely uses street attacks by the Apprentice Boys and others to exert political pressure.'

'Exactly! Look what happened to the Archbishop of York. Attacked in his coach to discourage other bishops from attending the Lords to vote against the junto.' Tom desperately did not want argue with her. Their time together was too valuable, but she should never have spoken to Culpeper. The fact he knew about the attacks on Bolton Hall made Tom even more convinced that his father was right about Puritan involvement, no matter what Culpeper told Elizabeth.

'Pym has used the mob,' she continued, 'but as part of a bigger plan, not to attack a family. Perhaps the first incident was by chance. A gang of Apprentice Boys drink too much in the taverns in Clerkenwell and go looking for trouble with the local gentry. After all, they only seemed intent on smashing things up. But then to return to steal Ellen? Why on earth would Pym do that? There would be no reason for it.'

Tom paused. He thought for less than a moment and then gave up his father's secret. He told her about the incident of the plague letter and the almost instant retaliation from Pym.

'Your father did *what*? Are you sure about that?'

His anger rose again. 'Well, if you wish to believe the word of Nicholas Culpeper over my father's….' She shook her head. 'No, no, not at all,' she murmured. 'Of course, if that is what Ralph told you.'

Tom expected Elizabeth to be angry but instead she was silent, pre-occupied. Their evening together was now beyond salvaging. He shivered and decided it was cold after all, and suggested they went back into the house.

Chapter 21

The Hop Yard, St. Martin's Lane, Covent Garden

Robert Petty frowned as he shouldered a path through the crowd in The Hop Yard tavern, carrying two mugs of beer. 'So much for somewhere quiet!' Petty shouted as he arrived at their table. He handed Tom his beer and leaned closer. 'Actually, it's the same everywhere! I checked a few other alehouses on my way . All are full. Something's up.'

Tucked away in a courtyard off St. Martin's Lane, The Yard was ideal for private meetings. Not too far from Westminster, Tom frequently used the small tavern to discuss matters with fellow MPs. But today it was full, with lively conversation increasing by the minute. He could feel excitement in the air.

Petty shrugged. 'To business. I have finally made some progress with my investigation. I now have the name of a person who I increasingly believe is behind the attacks on your family.' Petty's face was unusually animated, his deep brown eyes so often hard and intense, now flashing with excitement. Tom knew he would have spent many hours in pursuit of this potential clue. His heart sank at the prospect of telling his friend he had wasted his time.

'Do you know a merchant called Sir George Tansy?'

'I have heard his name mentioned once or twice at the Royal Exchange. No more than that.'

'Well it seems he knows about the Tallants…' Petty was interrupted by the sound of breaking glass outside followed by voices chanting: 'No bishops! No papist lords!'

'The streets are warming up,' Tom said.

'It'll calm down.' Petty replied. 'As I was saying, Tansy has been heard on more than one occasion complaining bitterly about your family and its ability to consistently source high quality spices abroad, and at prices which do not allow him and other merchants to compete. He is convinced you have insider information and is determined to discover who is providing it.'

'What kind of information?'

'He has not made that public, but he claims in the last six months he's received reports of two Tallant ships, one from London and another from Amsterdam, both seen returning from the China Seas, low in the waterline.'

'I find that hard to believe,' Tom replied. 'Much of the sea east of the Indies remain uncharted. It would be a severe and unnecessary risk to venture there when, to do so, you would sail past trading posts such as Bantam, where you could get all you needed.'

'I understand what you are saying but he is suspicious, particularly as one of the ships was Dutch.'

'So that's why he thinks we're working with the Dutch East India Company? It is as I thought. Guilty by association. I may have a Dutch uncle but that doesn't mean my family is working hand in glove with that company!'

'Yes, but...'

'In addition, I have received information from my father that convinces me Pym and his Puritan junto really are behind this. If I tell you, you must not repeat...'

He stopped. There was another sound outside. He strained his ears to listen above the tavern noise and heard chanting, by hundreds of voices. Petty had left the table to see more, when a man ran in. 'It's an army. They're on the march!'

Tom and Petty pushed past the growing crowd at the tavern entrance. They couldn't see the protestors but their rhythmic chant of 'No bishops. No popish lords.' reverberated throughout the courtyard. The word 'bishops' was followed by a handclap before the next words were uttered. That single clap by over two thousand hands in perfect unison cannoned off the walls and sent a shiver down Tom's spine. For the first time, he sensed the brute strength of the street.

The two of them worked their way into St Martin's Lane and turned right, joining the flow of people towards Charing Cross, which seemed to be the source of the noise. The air crackled with anticipation. They were forced to slow down as they approached the open ground around Charing Cross, now packed with people.

'By Jesu,' Petty murmured. 'The dam has finally broken.'

The crowd had grown into thousands, waving halberds and staves in the air, joining in the chanting. Many had makeshift flags and banners, held aloft above the smoke rising from a number of fires. Tom could also see sickles and hay rakes - the Kentish boys were there in force. He couldn't be heard above the chanting and cheering, so moved around the outside of Charing Cross, to where it led to Westminster.

The short December day was drawing to a close and hundreds of torches were now lit as they moved forward. Tom shouted in Petty's ear: 'I want to see what's happening outside Parliament.'

They set off down King Street, and saw stragglers among the Apprentice Boys walking towards them from Westminster. One group approached. 'King or Parliament. Who are you for? Tell me. Who are you for?'

Tom doubted if any were over 16. 'Lads, I warn you,' Petty said, 'leave the streets before you get badly hurt. The King's bullyboys are on the hunt and they're heavily armed. They won't think twice about running you down. Go home, while you can.'

The tallest of the apprentices stepped forward. 'Let them come. They can't stop us now. Not the bishops, not the Lords.

None of them. Filthy papists.' Tom had assumed the lad would be drunk, but now doubted it. His eyes were alight with excitement. 'We must save our country from Rome, and defend the King. Save him from his popish wife and her schemes.'

'What schemes?' he asked.

'She's in league with the Frenchies and the Spanish to send a popish army to England and bring back the foul old ways. And she's going to take off their heads in Parliament. Don't say she's not. It's true!' and he pulled a rumpled pamphlet from his back pocket and waved it in Tom's face.

He glanced at the news sheet, an absurd story claiming the Queen had visited the Commons, accusing MPs of treason. He told the lad it was untrue and ridiculous. It would never happen and, if it did, he would have witnessed it as an MP.

Tom had seen dozens of stories like this, the more fanciful, the more they were believed. Nothing he could say would change this boy's mind. The previous month he had found two of the staff at Bolton Hall reading a pamphlet claiming the Queen had bewitched the King through spells and potions to make him do her will. He told them is was rubbish. He could tell they didn't believe him but didn't want to argue with the master's son.

They left the apprentices with more advice to go home and continued to Westminster. Slowly, the road cleared and the noise diminished. Broken wood, stones and clumps of mud littered the surface. As they approached the Palace Yard, small groups of men were standing together, some injured.

A guard from the House of Commons walked up to him. 'I wouldn't venture any further, Master Tallant, if I was you, sir. We've cleared out the vermin, but there might still be one or two in hiding,'

'Who do you mean. What in God's name has happened?'

'Hundreds of those damn Apprentice Boys turned up, looking for trouble with their Lordships the bishops. They started to storm Westminster Hall but then turned their attention to the Abbey, threatening to pull down the altar and the organ. We kept them out but it was a near thing. They were breaking the front door to pieces when the scholars from Westminster College got on the roof and drove them away, throwing stones at them.

'That was the signal for a group of armed men to charge the mob, while they were in disarray.' The guard stopped and swallowed hard. 'I don't know who they were Mr. Tallant, or where they had come from, but to my mind those men were too hot, too eager, to draw their swords. They rode into the Apprentice Boys, slashing and stabbing, calling them round-headed dogs.'

'Who do you think they were?' Tom asked Petty.

'Probably soldiers of fortune returned from fighting the Irish for the King and now seeking employment, and trouble.'

'So, presumably, word of this attack has now spread and the people have turned out in force at Charing Cross to pay them back,' said Tom. 'My God, what a night this could be.'

Petty nodded. 'It's not a time to be abroad on the street. There's nothing we can do here. We must find a way back to your warehouse, warn the others and make sure it's secure.' and, wishing the guard well, they set off into the night.

After half an hour skirting around the centre of London, they neared Thames Street. Suddenly, Petty slid to a halt. 'Down!' he hissed. They both took cover and surveyed the lane ahead. There was something blocking its entrance on to Thames Street, with men carrying flaming torches visible behind it.

'If I'm not mistaken, that's a barricade across the end of Pudding Lane,' Petty whispered. 'Damnation. That means there may also be trouble up at the Tower. We'll have to try another way.'

They slowly retraced their steps and turned down a narrow alley on their right. The shouting, curses and the occasional drunken laughter became louder as again they approached Thames Street. Tom began to worry about the warehouse. They reached the end and, turning right, ran straight into a group of men coming up from the river, led by a large, broad shouldered figure.

'Aye, aye. What have we here? Two gentlemen out on the town?' A man's voice, threatening and surly, emanated from the dark. 'Job, bring that light forward.'

A small figure pushed through the group, carrying a branch of wood, one end wrapped in a burning rag. Tom recognised the familiar stink of burning tallow. There were six of them, some older than Apprentice Boys, and he sensed danger.

Robert Petty stepped in front of Tom. 'Yes, and we plan no trouble for you or your friends, so let us pass and we'll be on our way.'

'Plan no trouble? I should think not. Only the two of you, and no blades I can see, which is all the better, eh lads?' and as he spoke, the man slowly drew an old Rondel knife from his belt, the torchlight reflecting on its long blade and wicked pointed tip.

Tom cursed his decision to leave his sword at the warehouse. He had not wanted to attract trouble but now it had found them. These men were clearly not apprentice rowdies full of ale and looking for a ruck.

Their leader took the smoking torch and inspected Petty and Tom, who could now see the man's badly pock marked face, framed by greasy straw-coloured hair. 'Now, gentlemen. We are most grateful to our Puritan brothers for lately taking to the streets in increasing numbers. Normally I would regard this as a trespass on my territory, but I now see they provide cover for me and my boys to go about our business. Now we even carry a flame without notice, better to see who we're turning over.' The man laughed, a rasping sound like a whetstone sharpening a knife.

'Well, you're out of luck.' Tom replied. 'My friend and I have been to the local tavern but we never carry much coin at night, there are too many cutpurses in the city's alehouses. The little we have you are welcome to, but if you want to make your fortune you'll have to find other victims to prey on. So kindly let us pass.'

Petty reached backward in the gloom and gripped his arm hard. Once Tom had started, a deadly mixture of fear and bravado had loosened his tongue, like a boy who had inexplicably decided to poke a bear in the eye. The leader's face changed into a bleak smile. 'Can you hear this Billy Boy. The young pup can bark!' The gang laughed and a voice came out of the dark. 'Teach him his place, Jack. You'd do him a service.'

Petty leant back and whispered in his ear, his voice hoarse with tension. 'What are you doing? When I move, follow me, and run for your life.' The man momentarily glanced backward to talk to Billy Boy and Petty saw his chance. He leapt forward, punching Job hard in the face. The boy cried out and dropped the torch. In a second, Petty had grabbed the burning brand and buried its head into the leader's wrist, pushing and twisting to make the burning tallow stick to his skin.

The man dropped the knife, roaring in pain and slowly fell to his knees, gripping his right arm in agony. Petty grabbed Tom's collar and propelled him up back up Botolph Street, away from the river. 'Run!' he screamed and they both took off. He could hear shouts behind him but, pushing his legs as fast as he could, did not slow down to look back.

The outline of a church appeared near the end of the street.

'Quick! Over here,' Petty gasped. Tom followed down the side of the church into an overgrown graveyard, stumbling over lumps of fallen masonry. Petty grabbed his arm and pushed him under a tall gravestone that had fallen backwards against a wall. 'Quick. Get in there. And don't make a sound. Not even a breath, however long it takes until the danger passes.' And with that he disappeared into the blackness.

Tom crammed himself into the small space between the church wall and the gravestone, which acted as a sloping roof over his head. He strained his ears for any indication of the gang approaching above the shouts and laughter of Apprentice Boys roaming the streets. Surrounded by cold wet stone, his body began to shake.

Approaching footsteps. No voices. It must be them - disciplined, not a rowdy mob. They came closer. He heard a rustling noise. Someone was slashing though the leaves on the ground with a sword or knife.

A quiet voice broke the silence. 'I told you that was a mistake, to put out the torch, Billy Boy. Now we can't see a thing.'

'You shouldn't have dropped it in the first place. He pushed it into Jack, and the tallow was burning his arm! I had to shove him and the torch in the piss channel in the street, quick. You'll not like it Job, when he thanks me for it, you whoreson.'

The two lads continued their search for another twenty seconds before Billy Boy exclaimed: 'This is hopeless. They could be half way to Fenchurch by now. We need to get Jack to a physicker,' and he ran off, down the side of the church, back to Botolph Street.

By now, Tom was cramping badly and desperate to straighten his legs. The seconds ticked by. Then he heard a splashing on the stone above him, followed by a grunt, and a quiet voice.

'And I'll piss on your grave one day, Billy Boy. I will that.' followed by retreating footsteps.

Chapter 22

On the Thames

The winter sun glistened on the surface of the Thames. The air was crisp but had lost the biting cold of the last few days.

Elizabeth and Tom sat together at the stern of Jonah Dibdin's wherry in their warmest clothes, a rug wrapped tightly around their legs. They were making good speed to the south side of the river, propelled by Jonah's powerful strokes. Tom squeezed her arm and glanced sideways to judge her expression. He treasured his time alone with her and had suggested this outing to make amends for the terse conclusion to their recent stargazing. There would be no disagreements today and he was relieved to see a smile on her face as she surveyed the river.

'Where are you taking me?' her eyes alive with anticipation. 'I love a mystery! I know, we are visiting the Globe, yes?'

'I hope not Miss,' Jonah Dibdin cut in. 'unless you fancy shooting the bridge.'

Tom laughed. Jonah could be mean spirited and foul mouthed but he had got to know Elizabeth who liked his sardonic humour. In return, the waterman was always respectful in her presence.

Dibdin plied his trade on the east side of London Bridge. His fares would seek passage to the south side or further east, downriver - often merchants travelling between their warehouses and the shipyards of Deptford and Rotherhithe. It was a long haul, particularly against the tide, and the preserve of the strongest and most experienced oarsman, like Jonah.

If they needed to go upriver, travellers would catch a wherry west of the bridge, to avoid the force of the tide passing through its narrow arches. At certain times of the day, this could produce a massive surge of water, turning the river into a churning waterfall, with up to a six foot drop. This was known as shooting the bridge and, for all his experience, Jonah Dibdin would not risk it, unless he absolutely had to.

'No, we're heading for the south bank but on this side of London Bridge. Jonah knows where, so I suppose I should let you in on the secret.'

Elizabeth watched him like an eager puppy. 'Have you ever heard of the Pickleherring Pottery?' She shook her head. 'It's based at a place called Pott's Field which is near St.Olave's Church in Southwark. The pottery was established by a friend of my mother's, Christian Wilheim, who she met through the Dutch congregation in London. You've often admired the blue and white pottery on display at Bolton Hall…'

'Yes, Delftware. Do they make it at this Pickleherring Pottery?'

'They do indeed. Christian became so famous he became the Royal Gallipot Maker. After his death, his son-in-law Thomas Townend took over production. We will be meeting him today.'

'It is all arranged?'

'Yes. We will see their fine Delftware and I've asked Thomas to give you a personal tour, to show you how it's made.'

Elizabeth gave Tom a loving look. 'Well, this is prime! You know me too well, Thomas Tallant,' and she sat back in the wherry, her face wreathed in a beaming smile, closing her eyes to savour the fresh air and the regular movement of the wherry as Jonah rowed across the river.

He switched his attention to Dibdin, facing him on his rower's bench, his powerful shoulders keeping the oars pulling in and out of the water with complete precision. He enjoyed the silence, only punctuated by the creak of the oars and Jonah's steady breathing.

'I've been keeping an eye on your place.' Jonah suddenly

announced. Tom was surprised. Jonah was never short of a comment, giving full reign to his mordant wit, and would engage in conversations started by Tom. But he could not recall the last time he had broken a silence to make such a statement.

'What do you mean, Jonah?'

'I mean what I said. I saw someone by your warehouse a couple of times recently. Same person. Sniffing about. Trying to make it look casual, but I knew.'

'Knew what, Jonah?

'Knew they were up to no good. So I'm keeping an eye on your place.'

'Thank you, Jonah. But why didn't you tell me sooner?'

'And what would I tell you? I saw an ugly cove standing by your place? He didn't feel right. Not enough to take to the constable, is it?'

'So why are you telling me now?'

For the second time on the journey Jonah Dibdin did something Tom had never seen before. He stopped rowing, in midstream, for no apparent reason. He leaned on his oars as the wherry started to drift down river. His head dropped for a moment.

Elizabeth glanced at Tom in puzzlement. He leaned forward. 'Jonah, are you well?'

The oarsman lifted his grizzled face and there was moisture in his eyes. 'I may be, but my city ain't. There is a madness here, the like of which I have never seen in all my years on this river. The pride that people wear like a badge, the certainty they are right and the other man is wrong, on both sides, it is a black sin that eats at us all. And it can only lead to great sorrow. '

Tom was amazed. He had never heard Jonah speak like this, with the eloquence of despair, and it completely silenced him.

'When I see what's happening every day on the streets. Boys

attacking men of the cloth. Bullies hacking women and children with their swords. I don't know what's coming next. And that's why I'm warning you. And why I'm keeping an eye on your place.'

Elizabeth nodded her understanding and Jonah suddenly seemed embarrassed by his outburst. Her smile of encouragement seemed to increase his discomfort and he turned his head away, starting to row again for the shore.

Ten minutes later, they were walking through Southwark towards the pottery. They said little, her excitement doused by Jonah's outburst, which had caught them both by surprise. As the silence continued, he became exasperated. This visit was intended to make amends for the row he caused over Nicholas Culpepper. Now Jonah had destroyed the mood and Elizabeth seemed to be completely preoccupied.

She suddenly stopped. 'That's it!' she said quietly to herself.

'That's what?' he replied irritably. This excursion was turning into another disaster.

She gazed at him with a vacant expression. 'Did I speak? Oh, sorry Tom. I have been trying to recall something, and being on the river with Jonah has finally dislodged it from deep in my mind. I knew I hadn't imagined it.'

'Imagined what? I hoped you might be thinking about the secrets of Delftware.' He could hear the peevish tone in his voice, which annoyed him still more.

'Oh, I am. Of course I am .'

'So what were you trying to remember?'

'Now I've recalled what it is, I've realised it's nothing, even though it's bothered me for weeks. It happens often but, on this occasion, the irritant has not produced a pearl of wisdom. Come, let us proceed apace to the world of Delftware', and linking with Tom she strode towards St. Olave's Church which had appeared in the distance, her brow puckered with doubt.

Chapter 23

The House of Commons

Tom surveyed the crowded Commons chamber. Where was Barty? The air was thick with animated chatter as the room rapidly filled. At this rate, some members would have to stand. He was saving the seat next to him but could not keep it much longer. Several members had already requested the space and one, having then searched both sides of the floor without success, was now returning with an irate expression.

Then he saw the familiar head, bobbing and weaving through the crowd, working towards him. As he reached the bench Barty pushed in front of the other man and climbed into his place, ignoring his protests.

'I was beginning to think you were not coming,' Tom said.

'Oh, no danger of that!' his friend replied, out of breath. 'The crowds outside are tremendous. A lot of pushing and shoving. Pym has put his troops out on the streets again. I did wonder if I would get trampled underfoot.'

'He's building up pressure on the King,'

Barty nodded. 'By all accounts, protestors approached Westminster yesterday with another petition against the bishops, and were set upon by soldiers with swords. This time the troops were beaten back with cudgels, sticks, and stones, and the petitioners were reinforced by a group of sailors. In the end, Pym finally lost patience with the bishops and their blocking antics, so off to the Tower with them!

'Robert told me about your little night time adventure.' Tom smiled at the description. 'He'd never seen scenes like it, in all his years with the Merchant Adventurers. Meanwhile the lord mayor and the sheriffs are riding through London trying to cool tempers, just as the King orders the City's militia to defend his 'Royal Person'. I tell you it's chaos. And where is the leadership from His Majesty?'

Sailors on the march, bishops in the Tower, the militia mobilised – Tom had a sinking feeling that soon matters would spin out of everyone's control, and then what? He sat back, waiting for the Speaker to call the session to order.

Meanwhile, a mile away, Elizabeth Seymour was standing in Lucy Carlisle's parlour, feeling puzzled. She had been summoned to the Strand only hours ago. 'Most urgent' was the message, 'a matter of national importance'. Although Lucy liked excitement and intrigue, Elizabeth knew at heart she was a serious minded woman. Her concerns would not be based on idle chatter. The familiar rustle of skirts made her turn in time to see Lucy approaching at speed.

'Thank goodness you received my message! I'm not quite sure what I would have done if you had not.'

She nodded. Her mind was racing. 'What do you want of me?'

'I will tell all. However I must be quick. Time is of the essence.' Elizabeth sensed this was some sort of a test. If successful, would it secure her entry into her host's closer circle of friends and allies?

Lucy took a deep breath. 'Where to begin? Well, I was at the Palace this morning. Goodness, it is a cheerless place. No Christmas revels at Whitehall this year, I can tell you. I am there frequently and continue to enjoy the Queen's trust. She cannot sleep or think because of the constant noise from the crowd at the Palace gates. She knows about the attack on Westminster Abbey and fears the Palace will be next. And she believes the stories about Pym - that he intends to accuse her of high treason and wants her impeached. She is quite beside herself and, it grieves me to tell you, but I'm beginning to think she is losing her wits.'

Elizabeth listened closely but said nothing. She couldn't see where Lucy's story was leading, her words coming in a torrent as she switched her account from one person's actions to another. She re-focused her attention to ensure she missed nothing, especially any traps.

'Queen Henrietta Maria has constantly pressed the King to be decisive, to protect her, and this reached a peak this week when she demanded Charles impeach Pym and his acolytes. And yes, the King finally acquiesced and sent the Attorney General to the Lords to lay charges of treason before Viscount Mandeville and five members of the Commons including Pym!'

Lucy stopped talking momentarily to study Elizabeth. 'Yes, you heard me correctly. The King accused John Pym of treason. So why has nothing happened? Because both houses have, in effect, ignored his command. The Lords set up a committee to see if such a thing had happened before; the Commons said they needed more time for consideration...but both amount to the same thing. They've turned their back on Charles. Ignored his royal order!'

'What has the Queen said about that?'

'A great deal. As I said, I was in the Palace this morning, taking physic from my doctor to one of the Queen's inner circle, whose sister is ill. On my way through the royal quarters I could hear raised voices from the King's privy chamber. The door was ajar and I do not approve of eavesdropping but, where I was standing, it was impossible *not* to hear their majesties shouting at each other. The queen was furious, threatening to leave Charles.'

This is it, she thought with a growing sense of disappointment. We are reaching the essence now. And if it involves acting as a go-between in a Royal marriage quarrel, Lucy must find someone else. Elizabeth was not interested.

'Oh dear! This is taking me too long to explain, but it was necessary to give you all the information before asking you to undertake this task.' Her seriousness was confusing Elizabeth. Why couldn't she just get to the point?

'So the shouting continued,' Lucy said, drawing closer. The Queen could not believe Charles had allowed the five MPs to snub him. Instead of the Attorney General, he must go himself to the House of Commons with a troop of soldiers and arrest them. What was the phrase she used?...the King himself should 'pull these rogues out by their ears'! I thought that was rather good actually.'

'Did Charles agree?'

'Not at once, but the Queen was almost out of control, in a raging temper. If it was not such a dangerous move, I could believe he eventually agreed just to keep her quiet.'

'So when will this happen?'

'This afternoon, in only a few hours, so we haven't long.'

'Forgive me Countess, we haven't long for what?'

'To let Master Pym know, of course, so he and the others can escape the Commons before the King arrives.'

Elizabeth experienced a rush of emotions: astonishment, excitement and more than a little fear. 'But why would you help Pym and the Puritan junto? I thought you were firmly in the King and Queen's camp. That's why you wanted me to create a code, was it not? To write secret messages on their behalf.'

'Ah yes, I'm afraid I wasn't completely truthful in that matter,' Lucy replied. I have, in fact, used the code to pass and receive information *about* the King and Queen to and from John Pym. As a result I have been in a position to give her certain misleading suggestions. For example, it was I who first told Henrietta Maria that John Pym intended to impeach her for treason.'

'Didn't he?'

'I doubt it. Such a move could have split John's support in the House. Far better to put the possibility in the Queen's head, then see how she forced a reaction from Charles which would weaken his position still further.'

John? What exactly was the relationship between Lucy and Pym? She was struggling to keep pace with the flood of revelations. 'But your family connections to the Royal Court? Your own friendship with Strafford, the King's chief minister?'

'I know. It must surprise you but I have my reasons, which I will explain when I have more time. Now, we have to write a coded message which you must get to John Pym within the next hour.'

'Me? Why? How?'

'I cannot be seen anywhere near the House as I would attract instant attention. I cannot use a servant, it's too important. Your face is not known in Westminster. You wont be able to enter the chamber but if you give the message to the Serjeant of Arms for John Pym's urgent attention, he will deliver it. Do not entrust it to anyone else. Hopefully John will then have enough time to decode it and leave before the king arrives. Will you do this? '

She tried to ignore Lucy's eyes that were staring at her intently. With only seconds to choose, she paused and saw an opportunity. 'Yes, of course. But I need to ask you for a favour in return.'

Twenty minutes later Elizabeth was sitting in a sedan chair, swaying from side to side, as two of Lucy's servants trotted down the Strand to Charing Cross, carrying her effortlessly between them. They were not dressed in Lucy's livery and the Countess's crest on the side of the chair had been discreetly covered. She clutched the message in her hand. It was as brief as possible to reduce the time required to code and then de-code it.

She sat back in the chair and, entering King Street, passed the front gates of the Palace. She peeped out of the window, expecting to hear the clatter of hooves and see the King's carriage running before them in a race for the Old Palace Yard. Instead the road was clear but the ridiculous image of her trying to push past the king through the entrance of St Stephen's made her laugh out loud. She could hear the tension in her voice.

Lucy's servants lowered the sedan chair in the corner of Old Palace Yard and said they would wait for her. She got out, dusted herself down and strode into the House. The lobby was busy but she could hear voices from the chamber beyond. Good, the Commons was in session. She searched unsuccessfully for the Serjeant at Arms then asked a young man in a lawyer's robe. Apparently, the Serjeant was in the chamber and currently unavailable.

Elizabeth became anxious as the minutes passed. She heard a cheer outside and, fearing the King's approach, ran out to check. King Street was still empty but she knew Pym would need time to decode the message, once he received it. She had to act now.

Minutes later, she was returning to Lucy's house, the bobbing heads of the two servants visible in the crowd as they trotted up King Street carrying her in the chair.

Back in the chamber, one MP after another was denouncing the bishops in the Tower, but Tom could not concentrate on the debate. Time and again his mind returned to his encounter with the armed gang. Clearly not everyone wanted change. These street thieves liked things as they are – the constant chaos hiding their nighttime ambush of the innocents. He jumped when a Commons' clerk tapped him on the shoulder. The young man squeezed past Barty to whisper in Tom's ear. 'An urgent message for you Master Tallant, from a Miss Elizabeth Seymour.'

He froze. Why was Elizabeth contacting him in the

Commons? Had Bolton Hall been attacked again. Were his mother and father injured, or worse?

'Here, sir' and the clerk thrust a folded paper into his hand. 'Miss Seymour was most insistent that you give it personally to Master Pym immediately. She was very clear about that: most urgently, she said.' The young clerk bobbed a bow before returning to the lobby.

Barty looked quizzically at Tom who shrugged, turning the paper over in his hand. Sealed without insignia, Pym's name was on the front, but not in Elizabeth's writing. He lifted its corner but could only see numbers. What on earth was going on?

Tom would have to cross the floor of the House to reach Pym. It was customary for MPs to only do this between speeches, but her message was clear: the matter was urgent. So, with a sigh, he rose and stepped onto the floor of St. Stephen's. He noticed he was slightly crouching as he walked across. This struck him as ridiculous as it would make no difference to people's view.

There was a murmur of voices then the room fell silent. The MP addressing the house was staring at him. He raised his hand in apology and the man shook his head and returned to his text. Pym was frowning and muttering to someone next to him, and lent forward as he arrived. 'This is quite irregular, sir. If you wish to speak to me you should do so out of session.'

Tom kept his voice low. 'I apologise Master Pym but I know as little about this as your good self.' Pym appeared to be even more annoyed but said nothing. 'Someone I trust completely gave me this message to hand to you in person with instructions that you must receive it as soon as possible.

'You have not read it?'

Tom bridled at the suggestion. 'Of course not sir. It is private, sealed correspondence.'

'Hmm,' Pym muttered as he tore open the seal. The frown on

his face deepened. 'Come Denzil,' he said to the man next to him, 'we must leave the chamber immediately.'

He started to get up but then turned to Tom. ' I am most obliged to you, Master…'

'Tallant, sir. Thomas Tallant.'

Pym looked bemused. 'Ralph Tallant's boy?'

'The very same.'

'Well, there you are. Anyway, most obliged.' And turned on his heel and walked out.

Pym's sudden departure caused a stir across the room. As Tom returned to his seat, all eyes in the Chamber were on him. The debate continued, accompanied by the continuous hum of whispered conversations.

Ten minutes passed and there was still no sign of Pym. Barty spoke in his ear. 'Well, whatever was in your message has got his attention. Pym called this debate himself to hammer home the reasons for imprisoning the bishops. Why has he now absented himself?'

Following his father's advice, Tom had avoided public demonstrations of support for either side in the growing tensions. It would make it easier to be flexible during the coming events. He surveyed the benches, MPs huddled together, a number pointing towards him, and shook his head. Elizabeth, what have you done?

Then the voice of William Lenthall, speaker of the House, cut through the hubbub. 'I seek order. Order! As you know, the King yesterday commanded the arrest of five members of this house on grounds of high treason.' The assembled MPs erupted in a roar of dissent, shouting across the floor. The Speaker put his hands up for calm and gradually the din subsided.

'Order! I have urgent information, so I must have no further interruptions. Following the King's command, the House, believing this to be a breach of privilege, declined to hand over our five members.'

Lenthall paused to ensure he had complete silence. 'I am now informed that the King, as we speak, is sending a party to arrest the same five members...'

His next words were lost in a cacophony of shouting and stamping feet. 'I will have order!' Lenthall shouted. 'I must be heard!' Again the noise subsided to an angry chatter.

'And so, to avoid combustion in the House, I must ask John Hampden, Sir Arthur Hesilrige and William Strode to leave the chamber and join John Pym and Denzil Holles in a place of safety.'

Barty's mouth was agape. Tom wondered how Elizabeth had got this information and why pass it on? Several reformist MPs sitting nearby slapped him on the back and shook his hand vigorously. Amongst the confusion, a struggle broke out on the benches behind. William Strode was shouting furiously as friends tried to pull him from his seat. 'Leave me be. I will face the King's men and denounce them for the true traitors they are!' Other MPs remonstrated with Strode who was finally led away complaining bitterly.

By now many members had left their places to talk with others. Five minutes passed before order was called again. Throughout, Tom sat in his chair, stupefied by what he had witnessed.

A shout came from the rear of the room. 'They're here!' Then a clatter of footsteps and the sound of barked orders outside the chamber. The Commons instantly fell silent, members trying to hear who was in the lobby. An MP on Tom's left started murmuring to himself: 'There are hundreds of them. Papist rogues, desperate soldiers – come to cut our throats.'

Still nothing, then finally the sound of the lobby door slowly opening, echoing throughout the chamber. All lent forwards, straining to see who was entering the Commons.

A single person walked in. He took ten steps, paused, removed his hat and a gasp filled the room. The King.

Tom turned to Barty whose face was ashen. This was difficult to comprehend. He always wondered if one day he would see his monarch, but never imagined it would be in the Commons, arriving without invitation. The slight figure walked towards the Speaker's chair, looking to his left and right at the faces of the hushed MPs, his footsteps echoing on the stone floor. Surely he has not come alone, and he checked the doorway, which had been left open to reveal a large group of armed men waiting in the lobby.

The King stopped in front of Speaker Lenthall. There was total silence, an image Tom would never forget. A small man, the absolute focus of attention for the hundreds surrounding him, waiting as the mood became taut as a drawn bowstring. Finally, he spoke. 'By your leave, Mr. Speaker. I must borrow your Chair a little.'

In the midst of the tension, he was amazed by the incidental things he noticed: the King's perfect manners, and his Scottish accent.

King Charles stood in front of the Speakers' chair and addressed the members.

'When I called for the five gentlemen yesterday, I expected obedience, not a

m-message. I would not break your privileges, but t-treason hath no privilege.'

There was a murmur in the room. The King remained impassive. There was only a trace of his renowned stammer, and little emotion in his voice. Tom might have expected anger, given the King had been made to come to *them*. But if he felt it, Charles seemed determined not to show it.

'So now *I* am here, and I call again for those members to c-come forward and obey my summons. Gentlemen, I have accused these persons of no slight crime, but treason. I must have them wheresoever I find them.'

The King stepped forward and called out: 'John Pym'. There was movement as people looked around the room, but no response. The King turned a full circle, his head cocked to one side, listening.

'Denzil Holles.' Again there was silence. He tried to imagine the scenes if Elizabeth's message had not arrived. The MPs could not have resisted the arrest of the five, given the armed troops in the lobby. The King would have dealt Pym a dramatic and decisive blow – the capture of the junto's high command, but at what cost on the streets?

'John Hampden'. The King continued his roll call but his voice had flattened with disappointment. And with each passing name not answered, the silence was fragmenting into an angry chatter. In a matter of minutes, the King's dramatic political theatre was descending into a devastating farce.

When the last names were called, and no reply came. The King turned to Speaker Lenthall and asked where the five were. This will be interesting, he thought. The Speaker had not impressed in his dealings with him. He seemed weak to Tom and possibly corruptible. When Lenthall dropped to his knees, he expected the worst, but he was surprised.

Lenthall's voice echoed around the chamber: 'May it please your majesty, I have neither eyes to see nor tongue to speak in this place, but as this House is pleased to direct me. I humbly beg your majesty's pardon that I cannot give any other answer than this to what your majesty is pleased to demand of me.'

The King's head darted up and his body stiffened. Once again the chamber was held in a dreadful silence. Barty was sitting with his head in his hands, his body trembling. The moment had not been lost on anyone. The speaker had placed the rights and freedom of Parliament before the will of his monarch. And, in so doing, had publicly humiliated the King.

What would Charles do? He could not back down surely? Tom was betting the Speaker would be arrested but was mistaken again, as the King turned on his heel and walked away from Lenthall.

'Tis no matter. I think my eyes are as good as another's and…' and here he surveyed the benches for a final time, '…I can see that all my birds have flown.' And, at that, he turned towards the lobby, placing his hat on his head.

The King paused at the door. His voice was now shrill, no longer controlled.

'I do expect that you will send them unto me as soon as they return…if not, I will seek them myself, for their treason is foul, and such a one you will thank me to discover.'

And, with that, he stepped out of the room to an eruption of shouting, stamping and cries of 'Privilege! Privilege!

Tom sat back and saw his hands were shaking. The King's humiliation, the speaker's defiance, Barty's grief. He was overwhelmed by all he had witnessed, and, at that moment, recalled the Apprentice Boy outside Westminster, wildly waving his pamphlet in his face. The Queen had been to the Commons to accuse the MPs of treason. He told him the story was a lie. It would never happen.

But the lad had been right to believe. The world was upside down and his father's words echoed through the fog of his shock. The wrecking storm was upon them - a vicious, painful civil war, with no escape.

Chapter 24

The Tallant warehouse

Sam handed Tom the ledger with a smile on his face.

'I've completed the figures for the last three months. The storms off Spain disrupted shipments for others but came at the right time for us, with a full store. Prices at the Exchange have risen as supply tightens, and we've sold well. Pepper particularly is at a premium, the best for some time.'

He studied the ledger. It was gratifying to see how much they had profited. He smiled ruefully. In the past he argued for more trade in profitable spices such as mace and cinnamon, and less pepper, their staple. Ralph had disagreed, explaining that mace might make more money per sack, but they could sell a lot more pepper. If they held on until the price was right, it would make them more money than the others. Once again his father had been vindicated.

The good news temporarily lifted his gloom. Since he had unwittingly acted as Pym's saviour in the Commons, Tom had become a marked man. Traders he had worked with for years now turned their backs on him when he entered the Royal Exchange. Others pointed and whispered while a few shook his hand and congratulated him, which only made matters worse.

How had Elizabeth placed him in this predicament? He was about to send her a message when one arrived from her, requesting a meeting. She would be there at any moment.

He was in turmoil, his world teetering on the edge of a precipice, as was the whole of London. His father's growing enmity with Pym was pushing him into the royal camp yet Tom was now seen by many as the man who caused the King to be humiliated. And what did Pym make of him, the son of Ralph

Tallant, being his saviour? Might that inadvertent act be enough to broker peace between Pym and his father?

His head ached with it all and he longed to return to Southwark and the look on Elizabeth's face when Townsend had presented her with a Delftware jug at the conclusion of her tour. It had been commissioned by Tom, with her name painted around its lip.

He could hear Isaac welcoming her at the front entrance and steeled himself for the conversation that was to follow. She entered ,sat next to him and took hold of his hand. He looked into her remarkable eyes and his resentment slipped away. He just wanted to take her away from all this chaos, out to sea, the two of them free.

Elizabeth broke the silence. 'Tom I am most sorry for what happened to you in the Commons as a result of my actions. Lucy Carlisle has told me all about it. I did not intend you would be involved but it became necessary.'

He frowned at the mention of Lucy's name. The clouds started to gather again. When he spoke, he was surprised how much anger remained. 'Well if Lady Carlisle knows, so does the world. I can barely imagine the sport she has enjoyed at my expense, retelling my tale of woe!'

'No, please hear me out. Then we have something else we must discuss of much greater importance.' He smarted at her remark. More important than half of the Royal Exchange now treating him like a leper?

She pressed ahead, telling him the full story of Lucy Carlisle's coded message to John Pym, what it said and how it had ended in Tom's hands. When she had finished, he felt deflated, his anger punctured and his senses further numbed by this latest revelation.

'So Lucy Carlisle is now working for John Pym, gulling the Queen? More treachery! Jonah was right. We are being sucked into a web of madness!'

'I too was surprised to learn of this but have since discussed it further with Lucy, and can now understand her actions, to some degree. It might be difficult for you to fully comprehend, but Lucy Carlisle is fighting to retain her position as a woman in this man's world. She has been at the centre of affairs for over 20 years, and has come to realise that she is good at what she does. Influencing and persuading, greasing the wheels of diplomacy. Following the death of her husband, she was expected to dutifully retire to the country, but why should she? She wanted to remain a person of influence and, as it *is* a man's world, she had to play to her strengths within that world.'

'You mean her beauty?'

'Yes. She befriended powerful men like Strafford to support her so she could retain her place at court and remain a player in the great sport of court politics.'

'But now Strafford is gone.'

'Yes. I think that was a significant moment for Lucy. After his death, she began to suspect that Strafford, her great protector, had profited from land deals he had conducted on her behalf in Ireland. And she was disgusted by the King, how he went back on his word and abandoned Strafford to the Puritans. The two most important men remaining in her life – both made of clay.'

'But it was Pym who went after Strafford in the first place. How can she now bare to support him?'

'I know. It is cynical but she is honest about it. She sees that power is shifting towards Pym and needs his influence to maintain her position. She is using him, she does not hide that from me. But is he not also using her? And do not most men use women?'

What Elizabeth had said was not out of character but he was

shocked to hear her speak so plainly. Her conviction frightened him. It was alien to his understanding. It made him uncomfortable and unable to speak further.

She looked out of the window at the ships bobbing on their moorings, then turned to Tom. 'And there is more I need to tell you.' He almost flinched as she sat down opposite him and took his hands. 'This is difficult but I am convinced there is something terribly wrong with your father's actions at the moment. He is lying to you, I am sure of it.'

He sensed reality recede another step. 'What do you mean?'

'Remember my conversation with Nicholas Culpeper?'

Tom stirred and she took hold of his arm. 'Please listen to me. He didn't think Pym would be interested in raiding Bolton Hall. It's not how he uses the mob. After the second attack, I asked him to dig deeper. To find anything that might link the Puritan junto with the raids on your family.

'He trailed the length of Coleman Street, in the taverns and print shops, seeking any gossip, and came back with nothing, except several fleas in his ears for suggesting godly men would be involved in kidnapping.'

'But they don't know that Pym could have been provoked by my father's stupid idea to send him the plague rag?'

'It's a lie. Your father never did that.'

'What do you mean. He told me so, in confidence.'

'I am so sorry Tom. I suppose desperate times breed desperate measures. I know who created the plague rag, and it wasn't your father.

'What? Well then, who?

'John Pym was responsible.'

He was going mad. Was nothing what it seemed?'

'But why, how?'

'Let me explain. If you recall, it was the first day of

Parliament following the harvest recess. Pym desperately needed to get his returning supporters fired up, to keep the pressure on the King. So he staged a dramatic event to raise the temperature. He arranged to receive the rag during his speech. It was harmless – the only truth in your father's story. I suspect he knew Pym was behind the whole thing and, if so, the matter would never be investigated, so he was safe to claim responsibility.'

'And let me guess. Your source for this is Lucy Carlisle?'

She nodded.

'So I am to believe my own father is a liar, based on the opinion of Nicholas Culpeper and Lucy Carlisle. Have you gone mad, Elizabeth? Does my opinion of Culpeper and this dreadful Carlisle woman not count for anything? Why should I believe them, instead of the man who has raised me and guided my path through life?' He was shouting now. 'In fact, why are *you* believing them, knowing how much that would hurt me? Why have you not thrown it out like the horse shit it is?'

She kept calm but her face was flushed.

'Because I think your mother believes it too.'

Chapter 25

Bolton Hall

Four chairs were placed in the centre of the Tallant's spacious drawing room in Bolton Hall. Ralph, Tom and Elizabeth occupied three. The fourth was empty.

Ralph tapped his foot on the floor impatiently. 'Where is your mother? She said to be here at eleven. She didn't mention you both would also be present; and here we are, nearing a quarter past, and no sign of her.'

Tom shrugged. He wasn't sure if he had nothing to say or simply didn't know how to say it. At that moment, the door opened and his mother walked in. She looks strained, he thought. This will be a terrible ordeal.

Beatrix Tallant sat, nodded at Tom and Elizabeth then cleared her throat. 'I asked you all to be here because we need to discuss the recent events that have afflicted this household.'

Ralph interrupted, his face red with frustration. 'We've discussed this all before, there's nothing else to...'

Beatrix's voice cut through her husband's words. 'No. We most certainly have not been through everything before. You will let me speak.' The room fell quiet again. He had never heard his mother address his father like this.

'A young man has died defending our family. If not for him, we would have lost our daughter to a gang of kidnappers, and then who knows what? And our son was attacked at the family warehouse and knocked unconscious.'

Beatrix turned to her husband. 'You told me all our troubles are the work of Mr. Pym, aggravated by your decision to dose him with plague. But I am now informed, and I have no reason to doubt it, that you played no part in this so-called plague letter.'

Ralph was about to speak but Beatrix raised her hand. 'So, if our oppressor isn't Mr. Pym, who is it? Mr. Petty has come up with a name – Sir George Tansy. Apparently he doesn't like the Dutch and is jealous of our trading success. Well this at least seems possible, does it not? We've all met many Tansys in London. But he thinks we are in league with the Dutch East India Company and this is ridiculous. If I could have 30 minutes with Sir George, I could furnish him with many reasons why they are the last people we would deal with.

'Sir George of course is not to know this. But, even so, why should he invade our property? Why take the risk when he has nothing to gain? After all, according to him, our power comes from dealing with Dutch East India Company which, the last time I looked, was based in Amsterdam, not Clerkenwell. So, Ralph, what is actually *here*, in our home, that is attracting the bees to the honeypot? That's what I want to know, and Beatrix slapped her hand on the arm of her chair, looking straight at her husband, who stared back, stony faced.

'This is what I considered as I helped Elizabeth with her translations. As you know, I am rewriting correspondence and research papers from my fellow countryman Joan Bleau into English. His exciting developments in cartography are helping Elizabeth to develop her ideas on navigation. And you too, Ralph, have taken quite an interest in what she has uncovered, no?' He slowly nodded.

'Then an ugly thought formed in my mind. At first, I could not, would not, believe it. But, try as I might, I could not shake it off. Then two days ago, Elizabeth asked me a question. And my world went black.' Beatrix's voice started to break and she lowered her head. Ralph didn't move.

Elizabeth spoke next. 'Tom, you will recall that on our way to Southwark, I said that a memory had returned to me after our wherry journey with Jonah?'

'Yes, but it was of little consequence, you said so.'

'I did, because in that moment I could not be sure of its importance.

'Travelling on that wherry with you and Jonah took me back to that dreadful day when you almost drowned in the Thames and Jonah had to pull you out. I didn't want to spoil our trip to Southwark by mentioning it, but for the rest of the journey I tried to grasp this thread of memory just beyond my reach.

'Then, as we stepped ashore, it hit me. After your rescue, you were in a high fever for weeks. Later you remembered that Adriaan, the Dutchman who saved you with Jonah, had questioned you when you were delirious about a cart. Your father denied this but then you remembered Adriaan was talking in Dutch, and 'kaart' is Dutch for map. He was asking if anyone had questioned you about a map before you ended up in the river.'

'At the time, our focus was on your recovery and I thought little more about it. But then I remembered our conversation and how puzzling it seemed. Why would Adriaan be concerned about strangers looking for a map, and why had your father denied this happened? So, two days ago, I approached the only person who might have an answer, your mother Beatrix.'

She stopped and surveyed the room. Ralph was now on the edge of his seat, staring at his wife, who cleared her throat to speak.

'We need to open the windows and let some fresh air in, Ralph. Let's get things out in the open. I'm tired of secrets.'

'Don't, Beatrix,' he shouted. 'You don't know what you are doing.'

'Oh that's exactly what I do know. I have had enough of my family being torn apart by a piece of paper and the lies that surround it. Tom, your father has in his possession a map. There, I've said it, and the world does not seem to have come to an end!

'He told me many years ago it was an important map. He told me it was a rare map. What he didn't tell me was that others might come looking for it. Would stop at nothing to get it and that, even at the time you were fighting for your life in this house, having almost drowned, it would be the one thing on his, and Adriaan's mind!

Tom turned to Elizabeth. 'This is what you asked mother about the other day?'

"Yes, she did Tom'. Beatrix continued, 'because, God bless her, she's worried about the attacks on our home and on you. Elizabeth could not believe your father's cock and bull story that Pym being behind it, especially when she uncovered his lie about the plague rag. Who would? So she came to the one person she knew would give her a straight answer; and as soon as she mentioned Adriaan questioning you when you were delirious, I knew precisely why Jan was killed and Ellen almost kidnapped. It was that damned map!

So, where is it? I demand to know.'

Ralph lowered his head and closed his eyes. Tom could see he was weighing up what to do. Yes, that's right, make your calculations, father. This decision couldn't come from the heart, could it?

He stood up. 'Very well. Follow me.' His voice had regained its usual authority. The decision had been made. The mask returned. Tom was beginning to wonder if he could ever trust his father again.

He marched out of the drawing room, with the others in train. He entered a back room and, as he walked towards the glass house beyond, Beatrix cried out: 'Oh, Ralph. Not there. You didn't, did you?'.

Ignoring his wife, he approached a high bench covered in potted plants on the left side of the glass house, and lent forward. Using both hands, he felt under either end of the bench top and, grunting with effort, pulled upwards. The bottom of a panel beneath the plants slid out, revealing a cavity. He reached in and removed a long narrow box.

Without speaking, he carried the box into the dining room, followed by the others, and placed it carefully on the floor.

"We need our largest table to view this. Please could you clear the surface Tom?' A platter of fruit and vase of flowers were removed while Ralph unfastened the lid on the box.

Tom peered in and saw a large scroll of paper wrapped around a polished mahogany pole, covered in muslin cloth. Ralph moved forward. 'You and I shall hold one end of the pole each. Elizabeth, could you take the bottom of the map and pull it towards you? This must be delicately done.'

And so it was revealed, the largest map Tom had ever seen. Elizabeth removed the muslin and started unrolling the chart until it covered the entire table, reaching almost six feet in length and three feet wide.

The sheer scale of the chart was overwhelming. He was struggling to understand what he was looking at. He pointed to an area: 'Help me, father. This is land? And to the right, this is sea? Where is this?'

'It is a map of the South China Seas. Do you see these dotted lines across the water?'

'They are trading routes? So it's a navigation chart?'

'Yes. It's like an enormous rutter, showing all the established routes in the Far East. Like other rutters, it also provides distances, specific places to change course and by how much. But all the written information is in Chinese. Jonas managed to get a small part of it translated, plenty for us to explore, but the agent he used returned to China and has since died. So the map still holds many secrets.'

'It's extraordinary,' Elizabeth whispered as she bent down to study the land covered in trees and vegetation, all picked out in patient detail, and the blue sea, marked with billowing waves.

'It is, isn't it?' Ralph said. 'Hand drawn and painted, so please don't touch.'

'But where did you get it, father?' Tom asked.

'I knew a captain in the East India Company who had led one of their expeditions to the South China Seas almost 30 years ago. The Company was desperate to trade with China and lent large sums of money to local traders in the East Indies to establish connections. This proved to be a disastrous investment as, one by one, these traders defaulted.

'Each time a new expedition returned to the Indies, they'd find little progress had been made and the traders could not repay their loans. In this case the captain accepted the map in recompense from a defaulting trading company in Bantam. It was run by two brothers and, apparently, this chart is one of a pair they kept in their respective homes to plan and follow their voyages.

'The commander brought the chart home and, being an enterprising sort, didn't tell the East India Company. Six or seven years later, he fell out with them and left. He decided to realise some of his assets and offered the map to me. The price was substantial but I could see its enormous potential value.'

'It formed the basis of your father's partnership with my brother. Jonas provided the ships, your father the trade knowledge,' Beatrix added.

Tom was beginning understand the map better, as he examined it. 'This section at the bottom looks a little familiar. Is this Bantam? And, further over, is that the approach to the

Moluccas?'

Ralph nodded and smiled. 'That's part of the map we've been able to use so far. A lot of our trading in the past five years has come through our improved navigational knowledge of that area.'

Tom shifted his gaze to further up the chart, and whistled. 'And that's just the start, isn't it. Look at all the other routes spreading up to China. This chart begins where our current knowledge ends. It's our gateway to the East!'

'So you can see why no other merchant can ever get their hands on it.'

Elizabeth had been studying the map intently and now looked at Ralph. 'These round circles, covering the land, contain interesting symbols. Is this Chinese writing?'

Ralph nodded. 'Yes, we learned from the agent Jonas employed that they contain information about different cities and ports. It's an astonishing piece of work. Goodness knows how long it took to create…and there's two of them!'

'So where's the other?'

'We don't know. As both the brothers were bankrupt, I've always assumed the other map was also given away to clear the debt. But, so far, it doesn't appear to have fallen into the hands of an English merchant, thank God.'

'Ach, it is a pity. This map. So beautiful, but so dangerous. At least I now know why you built a glasshouse for my birthday,' Beatrix commented bitterly. 'How stupid I was. My pride and my joy, but only intended as a hiding place for your wretched map.'

'It was not like that,' Ralph retorted. 'The idea only occurred to me as we were building the walls and I saw the potential for a hiding place.'

'Anyway. It is not staying in this house a minute longer. I demand it.'

'But mother, I can now see why father has kept it hidden. With this map, and the secrets it still contains, the Tallants can become one of the biggest spice traders in the Far East. It is the means of our wealth and future success.'

Beatrix turned on him. 'But at what cost? It has already taken the life of Jan and what about Ellen? What would you say if I told you we could have a bigger house, more gold in the bank, be the envy of the City, but you could never see your sister again? I tell you now, if that map remains in this house, I will go. I will live with your Uncle Jonas in Amsterdam and take Ellen with me.'

'But that's…' Tom started to speak but his father interrupted, his face solemn.

'Your mother's right. The risk is too great, especially now its hiding place is no longer a secret. Just the four of us know, but it will only take one of the servants to see or overhear something and word will get out. We will have to move it secretly to the warehouse. Somewhere close and quick. Amsterdam is too far, now we know someone's after it. Too many opportunities to steal it on the voyage.'

'But the warehouse has also been attacked, father. And Jonah Dibdin, the boatman, told me he had recently seen two people acting suspiciously nearby.'

'Well, we have nowhere else, so we must take our chances. At least it will be nowhere near Beatrix and Ellen. I have no doubt that whoever is behind this will try again. They seem to know how much is at stake. I'm tired of this game of cat and mouse. It's time to confront our tormentors.'

'We should start with Sir George Tansy,' Tom said. 'I will send a message to Robert Petty immediately. Ralph nodded and carefully started to roll up the map. Beatrix, now quite spent, left the room, her shoulders slumped.

Tom exhaled slowly and saw Elizabeth staring out of the window and frowning. She stood and marched through the glasshouse to the garden.

'And I need a pipe.'

Chapter 26

London Bridge

The following morning Tom was standing at the northern end of London Bridge, waiting for Robert Petty.

Facing the City, he scanned the docks to his right, towards the Tower of London. He could clearly see Sam and Andrew at the back of their warehouse, preparing the wharf for an incoming ship. They were about a hundred yards away and he had the perfect vantage point to monitor any activity nearby, as he had hoped.

He could hear singing, rising over the constant hubbub of the dockside. Was that a psalm? Then he saw hundreds of people crossing the bridge from the south. 'My God, the Kentish Men are on the march.' He watched silently as row upon row reached the north end of the bridge and, walking past him, continued towards Fish Street Hill, bringing the surrounding streets to a standstill.

'Why are they here?'

Tom turned to see Robert Petty had arrived and was standing behind him.

'And what on earth is sticking out of their hats?'

'Hello Robert! I think these men have marched from Kent with petitions supporting Parliament against the King. They're displaying them to the crowd in their hats.' The orderly and sober procession was a powerful sight.

Tom took Petty by the elbow and moved him towards the wharves on the north bank. It was a chilly January morning and the two men had to bend into the stiff breeze blowing off the river.

'So I am to meet Sir George Tansy near the Customs House?'

'That is my intention, although he does not know it yet.' Petty replied. 'It's quite possible he would decline an invitation if he knew a Tallant would be present. So, I have told Sir George that, through my contacts in the Merchant Adventurers, I know a trader who wishes to discuss a business proposition. Sir George was most grateful and eager to meet. He has a meeting at the Customs House at eleven this morning, so I suggested an introduction in the nearby Bear and Staff afterwards.'

'Well let's see what he says. My plan is to provoke him sufficiently to anger him and hope he then shows his hand.'

Petty nodded as they strode along the wharf and soon the Customs House came into view. As usual, a crowd was milling outside, some carrying papers into the building, others deep in conversation with fellow merchants. War might be coming but trade in the Port of London showed no sign of slackening. As they approached, they turned into an alley running towards Thames Street and found the Bear and Staff nestling in a small courtyard on the left.

Tom was glad to get out of the bitter wind and they settled around a quiet corner table. He wanted to be nearer the fire but that was the busiest part of the tavern and he needed privacy. Petty went outside to wait for Tansy while Tom ordered some beers.

The scene was familiar. Groups of men huddled together, talking animatedly. But something was missing. He realised it was the sound of laughter. He was surrounded by serious faces, some anxious. The mood in London was darkening, he could feel it everywhere. He stood to greet Sir George as he entered with Petty. His face looked familiar but no more. No doubt they had stood next to each other on the trading floor from time to time. He was not a tall man and had a slightly pinched expression with small restless eyes. They exchanged bows while Petty got a goblet of wine for Sir George, who got straight to the point.

'Sir, Mr. Petty says you have a trading proposition to discuss. I am most eager to hear it.' Tom noticed his gaze was constantly shifting around the room as he spoke. 'He could not divulge your name, but now we have met I hope you agree that an honest conversation requires mutual knowledge of each other. I make no attempt to disguise who I am – Sir George Tansy, at your service,' and here he bobbed his head and allowed a shallow smile to fleetingly play across his face. 'I hope you will now feel able to do the same.'

His last words were a statement, not a question. Sir George was clearly accustomed to having his way, and Tom sensed impatience was never far from Tansy's demeanour. 'Willingly. My name is Thomas Tallant, merchant of the East India Company, son of Sir Ralph Tallant.'

Tansy was sitting with his arms resting on the table and Tom was prepared to seize them if necessary. He glanced at Petty, also ready to pounce. But Sir George did not move. His voice became passive, disinterested. 'And, pray, why on earth should I wish to do business with a Tallant.' The merchant grimaced at the mention of the family name as if he had discovered a bad taste in his mouth.

'Why should you not?' Tom asked innocently. Petty coughed into his hand to disguise a smile.

'Because I prefer to do business with honest Englishmen, people I can *trust*. People of good family and established reputation.' Throughout this exchange, Tansy's expression had not changed, but now he frowned and put a handkerchief to his nose. Turning to Petty he murmured 'What is the foul smell in

143

this room. Something degenerate.'

Tom would not be distracted. 'But I am English, am I not?'

'Oh come, sir.' Tansy replied, more quickly now. He's becoming bored and, hopefully, irritated, Tom thought. 'Would you deny the existence of your own mother. Given that she is of Dutch stock, I can well imagine you might wish to but, there it is.'

'And why do you dislike the Dutch so?'

'Don't act the innocent with me, sir.' Tansy's voice rose for the first time, a good sign. 'Why should any English merchant like the Dutch? You use any means to gain advantage over us, fair or foul, both on sea and land. Lend us money at exorbitant interest rates to bleed us dry. And your Protestant preachers spread the foul blasphemy which is currently tearing England apart.'

Tansy was now breathing more heavily, his face beginning to flush. 'And before you say the Tallants are different, I have eye witness reports of how your family work in league with the Dutch to line your own pockets: a Tallant ship leaving uncharted waters in the East Indies loaded to the gunnels with spices, sailing with another vessel under a Dutch flag. You trade in markets that are closed to us, or we don't know how to find. And how so, unless you have sealed a pact with the devils in the Dutch East India Company? The same devils who have murdered honest Englishmen on those very seas to satisfy their greed'.

Tansy swallowed the remaining contents of his goblet. We are closer to the heart of the matter, Tom thought. I must keep him talking. He must not leave now.

'I can see you are clearly angered, Sir George. Has your family suffered personally in this regard?'

Tansy pulled his head up sharply and glowered at him. 'How do you know? What business is it of yours?'

He continued in the same tone. 'I have no knowledge, only the sense of injury you clearly bear.'

Tansy paused, staring at Tom, gathering his emotions. His next words were spoken in a low, steely tone, brimming with hatred. 'Yes, injury indeed. And I'll tell you why. 30 years ago my grandfather John Tansy was trading in Batavia when, without warning or provocation, he was ambushed by a gang of your countrymen and brutally murdered. They escaped scot-free, and have denied any knowledge of it ever since.'

'How do you know the killers were Dutch?' Petty asked.

'Because one of my grandfather's partners who escaped recognised the language they spoke. It was Dutch, all right.'

'Well, Sir George. I am sorry to hear that, but I can assure you I've never been told any stories about such an incident in my family.'

'Well you would say that, wouldn't you? But why should I believe you, when you've already shown your Dutch Protestant colours in Parliament.' Tom coloured and glanced at Petty. His face was unmoved. Barty must have told his friend how he had unknowingly tipped off Pym about the King's attempt to arrest him.

'Yes, you turned the King into a laughing stock, didn't you, with your inside knowledge, no doubt gained as a Dutch agent in the court. Is that what you are?'

'Sir George. This is ridiculous. I was merely the messenger. I had no idea what was in the note for Pym.'

'But the person who wrote it did, and you must know them!'

He could see the meeting was not going to plan. Instead of catching Tansy off guard and pressing him for information, he was now on the defensive. Not for the first time, he fumed at Elizabeth for getting him involved.

'Anyway, it is of no matter. I made my mind up long ago to have nothing to do with any Dutch merchant and so I have no intention of continuing this conversation. Typical of you to get your ill-bred friend here', and he nodded his head towards Petty, 'to approach me with a fairytale about a business proposition. You clearly have no such thing. I have no idea what game you are playing *Herr* Tallant, and I'm not interested in finding out. Good day to you.'

Tansy rose to go but Petty grasped his arm. He recoiled from Petty's touch but couldn't free himself. 'Damn you, how dare you touch me.'

It was Petty's turn to show menace. 'Sit down, Sir George. For reasons I will not disclose, we are seeking a person who has reason to do harm to Mr. Tallant and his family. Given what you have said, it can be no surprise that your name was brought to my attention, hence this meeting.' Petty was staring at Tansy with a bleak, unnerving expression that Tom knew only too well and still made him uneasy, even when not directed at him.

'As you are a gentlemen, I will accept your assurance that you have no interest in Mr. Tallant, preferring to keep your distance. However, please do not make me seek you out again if I find this is not the case. You would very much regret it.'

Tansy stared at Petty and his hand, still gripping the trader's arm. Then suddenly he started laughing, loud and rasping.

'Oh Mr. Petty. You do not know what you are saying. Menacing people is neither my strength nor my style. The sight of blood offends me. If anyone in my family was inclined to avenge my grandfather, it would be my brother. For him, the injustice is still raw and chews at his innards. But don't ask me his name as I have no intention of giving you any assistance. As for his whereabouts, I have not the slightest idea. I have not seen him for over five years. But this I can tell you. He hates the Dutch with a passion. And he certainly is no gentleman.'

Chapter 27

Tallant warehouse

Ralph was at the warehouse when Tom returned from the Customs House with Robert Petty, who recounted their meeting with Sir George Tansy.

'Do you take seriously what he said about this brother?' Ralph asked.

'Yes, I do,' Petty replied. 'I was watching his eyes. They were steady and he didn't look away at any point. It's worth investigating further.'

Ralph nodded. 'Well you better be quick. I sense this storm over London is about to break. Pym and the other four have disappeared, probably in a hideaway around Coleman Street. The Lord Mayor has been attacked again for supporting the King. This time a group of women pulled off his chain of office, calling him a traitor to the liberties of the city. All the shops are now locked and guarded by their owners. And Parliament has mobilised the Trained Bands to protect them.

'I feel I'm on board ship, in the middle of an Indian typhoon, hearing the sails rip and the rudder begin to splinter. I know something's going to fail, it's simply a question of where and when.'

'You think the gang will wait until the next major riot then use it as cover to attack the warehouse?'

'I would if I was them. They've ransacked our home but not the warehouse yet. When they knocked you out, Dirck disturbed them before they completed their search. They will want to look again. If the city does goes up in flames, Thames Street will be choked with people, trying to get to the Tower. It would be a simple matter for a group to peel off from the crowd and head down the ginnel to our warehouse. And the street protests against the King would mask the noise of their attack.'

Tom was shocked by the likelihood of what Ralph had outlined. "And you still think this is the best place to store the map?'

'As I have said, I need to keep it close and cannot put your mother and Ellen in any further danger. This way we will flush out our tormentors and face them down. We can end it here, once and for all.'

Tom studied his father. His mind was still reeling from his discovery of the map's existence and the lies his father told to cover that up. He had a lot of thinking to do if he survived the next few days. But he understood the chart's importance and, despite his misgivings, he wasn't about to abandon his father in his hour of need.

'Then we better prepare our defences, hadn't we?' Tom said.' First, we need to increase our numbers. Father, can we spare anyone from Bolton Hall?'

'We have Dirck and you saw Mark gave a good account of himself. But we can't leave your mother and Ellen undefended.'

'But if they are attacking the warehouse, they won't trouble Bolton Hall, surely?'

'No, your father's right,' Petty intervened. 'They may first launch an assault on Bolton Hall as a feint to distract us. Your mother and sister would be there for the taking.'

'We must have Mark and Dirck from Bolton Hall,' Tom said. 'I will ask Elizabeth if mother and Ellen could possibly stay with her parents for the next few days. Then we can tell the staff to lock up the house, stay inside and don't stir until we tell them.'

'I agree, that's the best we can do,' Ralph said. 'So we have Isaac, Sam, Andrew, you and I, Dirck and Mark to man our defences here.'

'You can also count me in.'

'Are you sure, Petty? This isn't your argument.' Ralph said.

'Yes, I'm quite sure. An attack of a member of the Merchant Adventurers is always my business.'

'Thank you. I appreciate it greatly. We need everyone we can. So, your offer takes us to eight. Who else can we muster?'

'What about the crew from the Heron?' Tom asked. 'She docked yesterday from Antwerp. They're waiting to be paid, so won't have gone far.'

'I am loathe to mention our plight to anyone on the docks. There is no surer place for news to spread. We don't want to forewarn our enemies. The only one I would trust not to gossip is the bosun Henry Tulloch. I'll ask him.'

'I assume that's why you are not alerting the Merchant Adventurers, seeking their help?' Petty asked.

'Yes. We must deal with this threat ourselves. If we can put an end to it now, no one will know and the family's reputation will still be intact.'

Petty nodded and looked at Tom. 'Well, I know of one other who can be completely trusted and counts you as a true friend, and who would be insulted not to be asked'.

'Surely not Barty?' Tom exclaimed. 'With all respect, I'm not sure he is equipped for such a business.'

'In my experience this fight will not be a straightforward hand-to-hand combat. He is as capable of putting out a fire or bandaging a wound as anyone else.'

'And that would bring us to ten,' Ralph said. 'My lucky number.' The sardonic tone in his voice was not lost on any of them.

Tom picked a pile of sawdust off the floor. He poured it on to the counter top, evenly spreading it with palm of his hand, then drew the outline of the warehouse with his finger in the dust. 'So, how will we defend this building with ten men? There are two entrances, front and back,' and he drew a small cross in two places. The easiest access for the gang will be the front, which faces on to the yard and the ginnel into Thames Street beyond. They will need to get down the west side of the building from the front to gain access to the back . It's quite a narrow passage so we can block that .'

'What about landing at the rear by boat from the river?' Petty added.

'Yes, that's also possible but I expect it will be a night attack, when such an approach would be difficult. If we have time, we could also place obstacles under water in the dock, but that would be a lengthy and difficult business.'

'Am I right in thinking that, above the wharf where they would land, there is an open hatch on the second floor where you load pepper from the dock into the store?' Petty asked.

'Yes, it's directly over the landing stage.'

'Well then, I would forget about hidden obstacles. Block the side passage from the front as you suggest, but then make the rear of the building as welcoming as possible, by mounting burning torches on the wall, out of reach, so they can see the prize from the river.'

'Ah, build a honey-trap,' Ralph smiled.

'Exactly. Let them see we have a back door that can only be approached by water, and appears undefended. Do nothing when they land. Wait until they gather at the back door to break it down, then start the attack.'

'From the pepper store above?' Tom asked.

'Yes. You will need something heavier than sacks of pepper, but you can bombard them, and they can't reach you. With both the back door and the side alley barricaded, they will be bottled up on the wharf, prey to your missiles. They'll have to give up eventually and will be unlikely to return. Our rear entrance will be secure, leaving us to concentrate our defence on the front.

'And we will have divided their forces during the crucial first assault. By the time they are forced to leave the river and return to Thames Street, we may have sent the rest of the gang packing, with their tails between their legs.' For the first time in the conversation, he experienced a flicker of hope. The defence of the warehouse - perhaps it could be done!

'Let's now consider the front,' Tom continued. 'We have one aspect in our favour.'

'The ginnel?' Petty surmised.

'Yes. As we know, the only land access to the warehouse is through the ginnel leading from Thames Street to our front yard. It's only wide enough to take a two horse cart. Our end of the ginnel would be a perfect point to fight the gang.

'Yes, like the battle of Thermopylae!' Ralph said. 'A few thousand Greeks and Spartans blocked the massive Persian army by defending a narrow path which the Persians could only enter two of three at a time.'

'It sounds tempting but I would not advise it.' Petty intervened. 'We would need at least three people at this end of the ginnel who would require an escape route back into the warehouse if they were overrun. That could also provide an opening for the pursuing gang. No, we need to stick together, inside the warehouse, behind the strongest defences we can build.'

'Yes. On reflection, we all know what happened to the Greeks and the Spartans in the end, don't we?'

The silence that followed Ralph's question all but extinguished the flicker of light in Tom's heart.

Chapter 28

Tallant warehouse

Ralph walked briskly into the warehouse and called out for Tom.

'I've been speaking to my contacts. Parliament has set a date for the return of Pym and the four others to the Commons. It's only two days from now, on Tuesday. They're forcing a confrontation, to see what the King will do. They received a petition from 1,000 mariners, offering to protect Pym and the others on their return. The Committee of the House has accepted it and asked the mariners to sail up the Thames on Tuesday with guns loaded and primed!'

'That's all show, surely. They can't get past the bridge and up to Westminster.'

'Apparently, a fleet of smaller craft is planned, which will negotiate the bridge at the calmest time, on the tide turn. And the Kentish men will be followed to London by marches from Berkshire and Essex. It's all planned like a military exercise. The Apprentice Boys are unhappy because they've been told to stand down. The Puritans don't want any drunken indiscipline. This is it. The final assault. I'm convinced of it.'

'So they will build up pressure on the streets over the next two days in preparation, to unnerve the King and possibly force a rash move?'

'That's their plan so far and it's worked, so why change it? I believe we can expect our visitors either tonight or tomorrow night.'

'It's time to gather the clan.'

By early afternoon, most had arrived and were busying themselves preparing the warehouse defences. A wall of furniture, barrels and wood was growing inside the main entrance to the warehouse and all the downstairs windows were boarded up. The attack would be monitored and repelled from the first floor windows at the front and the second floor loading hatch at the rear.

The rear exit would be secured last, and Tom suddenly heard an unexpected voice from there. Elizabeth entered, followed by two of the servants from her parents' house, each carrying a large wicker basket.

She spied the barricade. 'This is a grim business. You really think they are coming?'

'We are as sure as we can be. We expect more trouble on the streets and, when it happens, it will be their perfect opportunity.'

She pulled Tom closer and whispered 'And the map. It is here?'

'Apparently so. Father won't divulge its location to protect us in case we are captured and they try to extract the information from us.'

'You can claim ignorance but it won't stop them trying. I believe he wants to be the only one who knows so as to retain his sense of power.'

'I know you have come to mistrust my father, but we are now all in this together. We must stick together.' She said nothing but he could see she was angry.

'Well, with that in mind I have brought my own contribution to the defence of the Tallants,' and she beckoned her servants forward with their baskets. 'Here is enough food and drink to keep you going for a couple of days and here...' pointing to the second container, 'I have something a little different.'

She lifted a cloth and pulled out a tube, wrapped tightly with a long stick attached.

'What is this?' Tom asked. All work in the room had come to a halt and the others were staring at the tube in her hands.

'The Italians call it a *rocchetto*, hence the English name rocket. It contains black powder which, when lit, creates enough force to propel it through the air. You'll have to take my word for that, as I have only had time to make six, so we can't waste one on a demonstration.'

He carefully picked up another rocket, examining it carefully. 'So, is it a form of weapon?

'They're designed to create fear and confusion rather than injury; to discourage, rather than disable. If you fire them from a first floor window, I am confident they will reach the entrance of the ginnel with a pleasing degree of force. You will need to make a simple device from two pieces of wood to rest them on and aim, but I can demonstrate that.'

'But how have you done this. Where did you get the black powder?'

'I foresaw you might end up in this situation,' she said looking around the

warehouse, 'and I had access to carbon and sulfur. That left saltpeter which would take time to source, so I started a while ago. As it is, I only had enough to make six and they're not as powerful as I hoped. However I wouldn't like to face one fired at me!'

'Where did you get the saltpeter?'

'From the stables at Bolton Hall and my parents' house. I asked the grooms to keep the old straw when they cleaned out the stalls each day. It is soaked in horse urine and a good source of saltpeter. But it takes a while to process. The quantities are small, but enough.'

Tom smiled at her. 'Thank you for this. We need all the help we can and these will give our enemies something to think about. But it will soon be dark, Elizabeth. You must return now to your home. I'm glad you've got the servants to accompany you.'

'Yes, and there's another guarding the carriage up on Thames Street. But Tom, remember - this situation - it is only a map. It's not worth dying for. I understand why you wish to resist any attempt to steal it, but there are far more important things to live for' and, moving forward, she kissed him tenderly on the lips.

They embraced and looked into each other's eyes. 'I will be with you again, soon. Give my love to mother and Ellen.'

'Do not worry. They are safe at our house. God protect you.' As she moved away, Tom could see in her eyes that she knew what was coming.

But it didn't. Not that night.

Barty had been the last to arrive, half an hour after Elizabeth left. He said the streets were full, more with noise and bluster than real menace. Tellingly, the Apprentice Boys were out in force making their drunken presence felt.

Nevertheless, they manned their stations: Tom, Sam and Isaac at the front first floor windows; Ralph, Dirck, Mark and Petty behind the barricade at the front entrance; while Henry Tulloch and Andrew readied themselves on the loading bay on the second floor overlooking the rear entrance. Barty was held in reserve to pass on information between the outposts and help with any emergencies.

At ten o'clock they reduced the lighting inside the warehouse and ate Elizabeth's food, before settling down for the night. Pairs took it in turns to keep a watch at the front and back while the others tried to sleep wherever they could lay their heads.

There was a brief alarm at midnight when Henry Tulloch reported a small boat afloat on the fringe of darkness surrounding the warehouse. Tom and Ralph ran to join him in the second floor pepper store but by then the vessel had disappeared from view and all was calm.

Slowly the constant shouts and whistles from the streets lessened and he began to relax. An attack without the cover of chaos in the city was unlikely, but they couldn't drop their guard and sleep proved elusive.

Clever, Tom thought. The longer we are constantly on guard, the more tired we will be when they eventually attack. Whatever the outcome, he wanted it over now. Then he realised what that could mean, shook his head and redoubled his concentration.

As dawn broke, the team of defenders stirred from their makeshift beds to discover snow had fallen overnight. Cold and aching, they huddled around a fire lit by Isaac in the parlour, extracting what warmth they could from the sulphurous sea coal struggling to ignite. Sharing Elizabeth's bread, cheese and ale, there was a companionable ruminative silence while they digested both their sustenance and situation.

When all had broken their fast, Ralph stood up. 'Thank you, everyone, for standing guard last night. We were not needed, but I am now more certain than ever the attack will be tonight. If not, we will have to rethink our approach. Thankfully, we should know, as the day wears on, whether tonight will see the resumption of the riots. If so, I feel sure our 'friends' will come calling.

'So, for one more day, I would ask you to stand guard. While it is light, some of you may wish to attend to business elsewhere but I would urge you not to travel too far and return immediately if you see any trouble. Otherwise, I will call another meeting at four o'clock, as the light fades. By then we must all be here, at our stations. Any questions? No? Then thank you once again. The Tallants will never forget your loyalty.'

The day dragged on, punctuated by news arriving, all of it ominous. Barty reported many reformist MPs were describing the King's attempt to arrest Pym as a 'traitorous design'. Of greater impact to Tom was the news that Philip Skippon, a skilled soldier and campaign veteran had been appointed by Parliament as major-general of the trained bands.

Petty said men from Northamptonshire and Leicestershire were joining others from Kent, Berkshire and Essex, carrying petitions of complaint for Parliament. Divisions were appearing among merchants about the impact of the trouble on trade, with both King and Parliament held responsible. Meanwhile Isaac reported that the talk in the taverns was of the Queen and her attempts to make the King and the country Catholic. Everybody, it seemed, had their grievances and villains, and all were spoiling for a fight.

As darkness set in, news arrived of barricades going up across the city, chains stretched across streets and pans of boiling water prepared to pour on to the heads of passing cavaliers. Tom could sense the moment was approaching.

To confirm his instincts, Ralph sent Andrew – their fastest runner – to travel the short length of Thames Street up to the Tower, to see what was happening. He returned fifteen minutes later, hammering on the back door. Tom let him in and he stood, bent over, hands on knees, gulping for breath.

'Get that back door locked, master. The Tower is surrounded, with more joining by the minute, lighting fires on the green. They're pouring up Thames Street from the City, and over the bridge from Southwark. Hundreds and hundreds of 'em!'

'Could you see any Apprentice Boys?'

'Not one.'

Without another word, Petty and Dirck dragged the barricade back to secure the door and everyone took up position. The waiting began once again, ten men now resolved, no longer uncertain.

Chapter 29

Tallant warehouse

'Fire! I smell fire!' Two hours had passed when the first warning came.

'Keep to your stations,' Ralph shouted as he ran up the steps to the first floor, two at a time. Tom was leaning out of a window, looking to his right.

'There's smoke coming from the stable. Thank God I sent Meg to Bolton Hall. They must have broken in. How did we not see them coming down the ginnel? Isaac, have you seen anybody entering?'

Before Isaac could answer, Barty ran into the room, breathless. 'The row boat has gone.'

'What do you mean?'

'I've watched the ginnel like a hawk Master Tom. Seen nothing,' Isaac replied.

'It's Henry,' continued Barty. He thinks a group of men have moved the Tallant wherry off the wharf into the water, at the far end of the dock. It's hard to see but he's sure it's gone...'

'Is the fire taking hold?' Ralph butted in.

'Should I change my position?' Isaac asked, looking gloomy. 'Maybe my eyes aren't sharp enough to be on lookout up here.'

A loud voice interrupted them, 'Well, our evening has only begun, and already our enemies have the upper hand.'

All turned to see Robert Petty who was standing at the back of the room, surveying the scene.

'The gang has planned and prepared the ground well. I suspect they entered the yard today when our guard was down and hid in the stable, probably the hayloft, waiting for darkness before getting to work. The fire was meant to distract us while they took the boat. We should have used it to buttress the barricade down the side alley. It would have been of more use there.

'They're sending a signal – no escape. Trying to disorganise and unnerve us and, from what I can see, they're succeeding,' Petty warned. 'Many a battle is lost through confusion. We must keep our heads and only communicate what is necessary, when necessary. And we should assume that a number of the gang are now outside our walls, and following their plan to hit us at different points, probing for a weakness.'

The silence that followed Petty's assessment was broken by loud cheering from the street and chanting of 'No Papists! No Papists!''You've all heard what Robert had to say?, Tom shouted out. 'Back to your stations and let's see these whoresons off the premises!'.

He approached Petty. 'Well said, Robert. I am glad of your experience.'

'My experience did not prevent them slipping in today, did it? It could be a long night. Pray for more snow, and a clear sky. We'll have a better chance of spotting them in the moonlight against the white ground.'

'Still no movement at the ginnel, Isaac?' Ralph called out.

'Nothing I can see,' Isaac replied, sounding downcast.

'Well that's good enough for me. You had the sharpest eyes on board when we sailed together, even better than mine,' and he winked at Tom.

'What's that sound?' Petty put up his hand and leaned out of the window. Instead of looking forward, he shifted his gaze directly below him, trying to make out possible movement.

'Well, the little bastards…'

Petty signaled Tom to join him. 'I'm glad we barricaded both inside and outside the front entrance. There are two of them, behind the ship's timbers piled in front of the door, trying to move them. They're creating a clear run at the door for their mates waiting in Thames Street.'

'With a battering ram?'

Petty nodded. ' I suspect so. Let's warm things up for them, shall we? Sir Ralph. If you are returning to your station guarding the front door, could you ask Dirck to join us? I have a job he will relish.' Tom's father smiled and patted the mound of cobbles in the corner of the room as he walked past.

Dirck arrived and was shown his target. A grim smile came over his face as he approached the window, a cobble in each hand. Leaning out, he unleashed a stone into the gloom below. It hit one of the timbers, as did the second. 'I am getting my aim', Dirck said. 'The next two are for Jan', and leaning forward he hurled a third stone. There was a cry below and a flurry of movement followed by an agonised scream when the fourth cobble also found its mark.'

A voice cried out: 'Clem! Clem! Let him have it. He's killing us!' as Dirck turned towards the window again, re-armed with stones.

'No Dirck!' Tom shouted and threw himself at the Dutchman, pushing him to the floor. At the same moment there was a sharp crack on the stone window frame and a shower of dust.'

'They've got a musket,' Petty warned. 'Step back from the windows. Put out the lanterns! We will have to work by candlelight and not show ourselves. It will make…'

'Tom, Tom,' Barty was running down the stairs calling softly.

'Keep down! What is it?'

'It's begun as Robert described. There are four of them prowling around the back door like wharf rats. Henry is preparing our welcome.'

He left Petty and Dirck to continue their bombardment and followed Barty to the pepper store. He nodded at Tulloch and Andrew as he approached the open loading bay. Peering over the edge, he could see four shadowy figures working silently below. Two disappeared down the side alley and returned minutes later, whispering something to the others, pointing towards the alley and shaking their heads.

Tom waited. He wanted them grouped together by the back door before taking action. Tulloch and Andrew now had six bags propped up next to the loading bay, waiting for his signal. Each sack carried a heavy load of wet sand and shingle from the shoreline. He checked again and heard grunting below as the men started pushing at the back door.

He stepped back and nodded to Tulloch. The bosun grabbed a sack and launched it over the edge of the loading hatch. There was barely time to hear the crash before Andrew followed with a second. In his eagerness, he forgot to let go. Tom grabbed him just before he disappeared through the loading bay with the sack.

Henry and Andrew didn't let up until all six bags had reached their target. Hearing low moans from below, they peeped over the edge to see two men helping a third limp back to their boat. A fourth was following, holding his head.

He slapped Tulloch and Andrew on the back. 'Well done, men,' he whispered. 'So far, so good. Stay alert.'

As he left the pepper store, he counted another eight sacks ready for use. They had decided to make the first bombardment as terrifying as possible. He now prayed they had enough in reserve, in case the gang came back for another attempt.

He ran down to the first floor and gave Petty a nod. 'Have they retreated up the ginnel, Robert?'

'The two at the front? Yes. One had to be supported by the other. They'll be reporting back to the gang leader.'

'And soon he'll find his sea borne assault's been repelled,' Tom grinned. 'A heavy broadside from Andrew and Henry

Tulloch was enough to sink 'em!'

'I hate to spoil the good news, Master, but I think you should see this.' Sam was crouching by one of the windows. He moved aside allowing Tom to peer to his right over the window ledge. 'Quickly, fetch my father' he told Sam.

Ralph arrived and spent several minutes by the window studying the stable roof which was now well alight, flames licking up the side of the warehouse. He was careful not to put himself on show. They still did not know the whereabouts of the man with the musket.

He turned to Tom. 'People said I was mad when I used stone from the old monastery at Bolton Hall to rebuild the warehouse. It took two years, carting it from Clerkenwell and cutting it at the docks, but now I thank God I did. That wall will hold and give us time. The roof, however, is another matter. It is much higher than the stables, and we've had such a wet December. The tiles and beams will be well doused by the recent rain and now this snow, but it will not last forever. But remember, they can't afford to burn us out. They want the map intact.'

Chapter 30

Tallant warehouse

There was a lull after the first attack and the defenders took the opportunity to get a mouthful of food and drink. Their respite was brief.

'We have more visitors on the wharf,' Barty reported. Tom ran to the Pepper Store and saw four shadowy figures scouting the rear of the building. They were avoiding the back door, which was surrounded by sacks, their split sides spilling wet sand and stones across the wharf. One of the men went down the side alley and returned minutes later, walking past the other three back to their boat, disappearing into the gloom.

'What are they up to this time?' he murmured to himself. 'Henry and Andrew, get another four sacks ready.' Once those had gone, only four bags would remain, enough for one final salvo. This next attack must be repulsed forcefully. The men below seemed to be waiting but finally approached the back door. Two of them tried to move the sacks on the floor to one side while the other stood back watching the loading bay above.

'Get ready,' he whispered to the others. Henry Tulloch picked up a sack and dragged it to the edge of the opening. Tom saw the guard below look down and move towards the other men. 'Now Henry!' he whispered hoarsely .

Henry dragged the sack into the opening. There was a noise and the bosun recoiled with a cry and let go of his load, which tumbled out of the bay, missing its target. Tom scrambled towards the injured man, who was writhing on the floor.

'They've shot me, those whoresons, in the shoulder...left

shoulder. Jesu, it hurts.'

Tom took a handkerchief from his pocket. 'Press this against the wound. We'll move you somewhere safe in a minute.' He turned to Andrew. 'They must have transferred the musket from the front to the back, over the alley barricade, unless they've got two. Come on, we've got to continue while they're reloading.'

Andrew didn't move. He was staring at Tulloch with his mouth open. 'Andrew!' Tom shouted. 'Help me, come on!' and he seized a bag and, glancing below, launched it over the edge. The young groom was now at his side, next sack in hand. He grabbed it and, in one movement, hauled it through the gap to the ground below. There was a satisfying howl of pain. One sack left. Did he have time before the musket was ready to fire again? Only one way to find out, and, keeping as far back as he could he flung the heavy sack with his remaining strength.

He heard a whistle as a musket ball flashed past his face and the thud as it hit the roof beam behind him. Tom flung himself to the floor. He saw his final sack was teetering on the edge of the open hatchway. With a smile he stood, retrieved the bag and dragged it to the lip of the hatch. Unhurried, he surveyed the scene below. All three men were at the entrance, hammering and pushing at the door.

Tom hesitated. He was seconds from possibly killing a man. Then he thought of Jan, casually knifed in the side, and that he too would now be dead if the musket shot had been two inches closer. He pushed his doubts to one side, took deliberate aim and carefully dropped the full weight of the sack on to the nearest figure. The man crumpled to the ground without a sound, sending the other two running back to their boat. Would that make the raiders give up? His hopes rose as the minutes passed. Then, with relief, he saw the fallen figure on the wharf stirring. In his heart, he knew he wasn't a killer. Reassured, he was about to get help for Henry when a movement caught his eye. The two men were charging out of the gloom towards the warehouse as fast as possible, followed closely by a third.

His heart sank. 'They're determined to get past us, and we've only four sacks left. We are running out of ammunition and they have all night to get through.' The thought overwhelmed him. He turned to Andrew. 'You better move Henry to my bed. Get Barty to help you. I'll do what I can to keep our friends below at bay.' Tom suddenly wished Elizabeth was there to help him. He badly needed her calm confidence and quick thinking. She'd know how to get out of this mess.

Andrew didn't move. He was staring through the hatch, pointing. 'M...master. Look!'

'Yes, I know. They're attacking again. We need to find Henry somewhere safer, so get a move on.'

'No, master. Look!' and he grabbed his shoulder and pointed.

Tom peered into the gloom and caught his breath. Another seven men had appeared out of the dark, following the three who had now reached the warehouse. Two of the seven were holding flaming torches while their leader was striding purposefully forward, swinging a wooden post in large, strong hands, and rolling his massive shoulders.

He knew the game was up. Once they ran out of sacks, this group would make short work of the rear door. Then, all that remained would be the make-shift barricade on the other side. In a matter of minutes, they would be inside and raising hell. With a heavy heart, he realised they would have to surrender, if they were allowed to.

He was about to run downstairs but something about the leader made him stop. He inched closer to the entrance to get a better look and was astonished to see the man approach one of the gang and fell him with a single blow of his wooden cudgel. He glanced up at Tom, grinned and put his thumb up.

'Jonah!' he cried out. 'It's Jonah Dibdin! By all the saints!

What's he doing here?'

Jonah ignored him and turned to the pair of remaining attackers. 'Right. As I see it, you two have a choice, which is a rare thing in my world, so make the most of it. Either you leave here now and not return, and tell your other friends likewise. Or you can be a brave pair of bullies and try your luck against the seven of us. So, what's it to be?'

The two men exchanged glances and their shoulders dropped. They put their hands up. One spoke up. 'But how can we leave? You've stolen our boats.'

'And my musket,' added the other.

'It's not too far to swim,' Jonah said. 'Once you're in the river, head for the bridge. You'll pass some landing steps on the way. But I wouldn't hang about. More than ten minutes in the drink in December will finish you off.'

The first man pointed at the two members of the gang felled by Tom's sack of sand and Jonah's cudgel. Both were now sitting up but still groggy.

'Leave them. They've nowhere to go, so I'm sure Master Tallant above will make them very welcome when your little party is over. So, off you go boys. Enjoy your dip.'

'But I cannot swim!' one of them said.

Jonah sidled up to the man and pushed the end of the cudgel into his chest before leaning into his face. 'I'll let you into a little secret, my son. Neither can I.' Jonah laughed and turned to the boatmen. 'Get rid. I can't stand the sight of them,' and the two men were grabbed by the arms and marched off towards the quay, protesting loudly.

Jonah finally turned to look up at Tom who had witnessed the whole scene. 'Well, this is a fine pickle, even for you, if I may say so. Mind you, the whole of London is going to hell in a handcart tonight, without the plague. The city is doing itself in, all on its own, quite nicely.'

'The streets are in disorder?'

'Everywhere. It's Bedlam.'

'But why are you here, Jonah?'

There was a shout of alarm from the wharf and then several loud splashes. Jonah didn't react.

'As I told you the other day, I have no truck with either side in all this trouble. I take the fare and keep my mouth shut. But it's plain to me that a lot of people are using the current rumble for their own profit, and that brings misery on us all. And when they step into my backyard to play their games, I won't have it.

'And my friends here, we all feel the same, don't we boys?' There was a murmur of agreement among the other boatmen who were wearing their distinctive red jerkins carrying the badge of the watermen. They look like an army, Tom thought.

'So tonight we decided to patrol the north shore in our wherries. Then we heard that churl, now trying to stay afloat in the river, firing off his musket, so we came to have a looksee. When I saw it was your warehouse I thought 'well, I better save this fare – he's too good a tipper' and so here we are. Easy as wink to sneak up on the shooter and grab him. The rest you saw.'

Once again, Tom felt his hopes rise. Seven more handy men on their side could tip the balance. 'I can't thank you enough for rescuing us Jonah, as we're under attack at the front of the warehouse as well.'

'Before you start getting ideas, I don't know what your fight is with these folk,' pointing at the two still sitting on the floor, 'or any of their friends, and I don't want to.

'I have a living to make on this river and a reputation to keep. If I kept wading into people's disputes, taking sides, I'd be out of business before I knew it. I'll always defend the river, like tonight. Always. But I can't take on your trouble. I'll guard your back door if you like. No-one else sets foot on this wharf tonight, I promise you that. So you'll have a way out if things get too tasty. But don't ask for more.'

Tom felt disappointment, but securing one of their two fighting fronts would help greatly.

'Jonah. I understand your position and thank you again.'

'Anyway, what you need is to get at this gang from the rear, from Thames Street. And that's not happening. Not by us or anyone else. They've got the street stitched up tight.'

He waved to Jonah and returned to the ground floor. There had been no further attacks at the front of the warehouse.

Chapter 31

Tallant warehouse

His father was astonished. 'Jonah Dibdin? Our saviour? I don't believe it!'

'He says he's defending the river, father, and I know what he means. He ferried Elizabeth and I last week and was deeply troubled by the current turmoil. He sees his London, his way of life, slipping from him.'

'Well, whatever his reasons, I'm grateful for his intervention and will tip him more generously in future, if we ever get out of this mess. I think we've given Tansy's men, or whoever is behind this, a bloody nose and they have withdrawn to regroup. They'll soon find our back door has been slammed shut for the night. That may change their thinking. Then again, they may decide to wait for the fire to do its work.'

Tom looked through the window. The stable roof was well alight, flames climbing further up the stone warehouse wall. There was no sign of smoke yet from the roof above but the external timbers supporting the tiles were blackened. If they could just hold on until the stable burnt itself out, they'd have a chance. But if the warehouse roof started to catch, it could spread in minutes.

Tom went to check on Henry Tulloch, lying on his bed, clutching his shoulder and sweating. Barty was sitting next to the bosun feeding him brandy from a glass.

'Thank you, Sir, that is helping the pain,' and leaning forward he took another swallow. Barty gently lowered Henry back on to his pillow, turned from the bed to stand close to Tom.

169

'As you can imagine, I have no idea what I'm doing, other than keeping this poor man as comfortable as possible. I have made one medical examination however. Something I remember Elizabeth talking about a while back. I gently turned Mr. Tulloch onto his back and saw nothing.'

'No exit wound?'

'Quite. I am not sure if this constitutes good or bad news – Elizabeth didn't tell me that, or perhaps I wasn't listening – but I suspect it's not good. Infection?'

'Yes, eventually. But for now we've done what we can. Has the bleeding stopped?

'Mainly, but the injury is clearly giving him a great deal of pain, hence my liberal doses of your brandy.'

He squeezed Barty's arm and said: 'I can see he is in good hands. Do you…'

His father's voice broke in. 'Tom. Tom. To the front, now!'

He raced to join him and followed his gaze. 'Keep an eye on the mouth of the ginnel. Watch. There! Can you see?'

Ralph Tallant was famed among merchants for his sharp vision. He was still the first on board ship to spot a sail on the horizon, and he was right again. In the gloom, Tom saw someone scamper out of the ginnel on all fours and into a dark corner of the yard.

'That's the third by my reckoning. They're building up numbers for a mass attack on the front. We can repel a handful of them, but if they gather in numbers out of sight and then come at us, throwing stones won't be enough. We might wound a few but the others will pull down the barricade and then they'll bring up the ram. While they hide in dark corners, we can't reach them. Maybe we'll need Dibdin's back door after all,' he said gloomily, suddenly deflated.

There was a cough behind them. Both turned to see Sam, holding in his hand a *rocchetto*. 'Begging your pardons, sir, but perhaps Miss Elizabeth had just such a contingency in mind?' In the frenzy of the fight, Tom had completely forgotten about her contribution to their defence. It was worth a try.

'Quick. Pull the loading ramp up to the window and pass me a candle.'

Sam scampered off and returned with the simple wooden mechanism Elizabeth had devised. Tom examined the two pieces of wood, nailed together to form a V-shape. They had been rubbed smooth to form a four foot long shallow channel for the rocket to travel along.

Taking care not to be seen, he propped one end of the ramp on the edge of the open window and carefully took the first rocket from its basket and placed it on the other end. He sighted down the length of the ramp and pointed it towards the corner where the attackers were gathering. He watched his father for approval but Ralph simply shrugged his shoulders. Remaining at the end of the ramp that housed the rocket, he reached down and picked up the lit candle. He gently moved the flame towards the fuse. He could feel the sweat on his brow and the candle starting to tremble as he held the flame still closer.

Sam grabbed his arm. 'Stop, master! Stop!' Tom jumped and dropped the candle on the floor.

'Did you not hear Miss Elizabeth's instruction? She said on no account be behind the *rocchetto* at the moment it is lit!'

A wave of relief washed over him. 'Thank you, Sam. You are right. I was so nervous, I had completely forgotten. If this device inspires half as much trepidation in the enemy as it does in me, it will serve us well' and, still holding the ramp, he moved to its side.

Ralph picked up the candle which was still alight. 'Come Tom, more men have left the ginnel. We need to see if this invention of Elizabeth's will work or not.'

'Oh I have no doubt it will work, knowing her as I do, and

that's what worries me, because I have no idea what is about to happen!' And with that, he took the candle and, standing sideways on, plunged it into the twisted taper of paper at the end of the rocket.

Everyone in the room stood waiting, Isaac behind a barrel, ready to duck.

Tom tried to hold the ramp steady, still pointing at its target. He removed the candle and the paper started to smoke. The end started to glow red, but then to dim. In exasperation, he lent forward and blew on the glowing taper. It began to crackle then his world disappeared in a flash of white light and choking smoke. He fell to the floor and rolled away from the launch ramp. A cheer erupted in the room and he gingerly picked himself up. His skin was hot and he could smell singed hair among the stink of burnt black powder.

His father emerged through the fog of smoke, grinning broadly. 'That young lady of yours never ceases to amaze me Thomas! Come and see.' Ralph led him by the arm to the window. There was a glowing mark in the wall above the corner of the yard where the gang members were hiding, and the sound of commotion below.

'When the rocket lit, it emitted a great deal of fire and smoke from its rear, like the very Devil himself, and after trembling for a second or two it shot off the ramp into the night sky. By then, you had dropped the ramp so the rocket was aimed too high, but it dipped at the last minute and hit the wall above those rascals with a tremendous shower of sparks. By its light I could see five or six men cowering in the corner and there were shouts of alarm. If we can aim the next one a little better, we will send them running, I'm sure!'

Tom nodded. He picked up the ramp again, placed another rocket and aimed it at the corner of the yard. He noticed that Petty and Dirck had now entered the room to watch. He picked up the candle and lit the fuse. As soon as he saw it glow, he turned his face and stretched his neck as far away from the ramp as possible. The rocket ignited and in a cloud of flame and smoke took off. Tom twisted his head back in time to see the missile leave the window. It shot off across the yard but, this time, fizzled out and dropped to the ground, short of its target.

There was a sigh of disappointment in the room, but he could see the failed attempt had still caused consternation outside. He could sense the tide turning so grabbed the ramp, loaded it and took careful aim. Seconds later the rocket was alight and this time flew straight and true, deep into the group of men hiding in the corner. There was a scream and, as the smoke cleared, Ralph shouted 'they're on the run, like frightened rabbits.'

Sure enough, Tom watched the mouth of the ginnel and saw dark shapes pushing and shoving, trying to escape back on to Thames Street. The room erupted in cheers. Petty slapped him on the back but he was too busy to notice, preparing the next rocket.

'Thanks to Elizabeth, we have the upper hand for the first time.' Tom shouted across the room. 'Now we must keep it. We need to move the ramp and line it up on the entrance to the ginnel. As soon as one rabbit pokes its head out of the hole, we'll send a rocket up its arse!' There was another cheer and he caught sight of his father, smiling and nodding.

He lined up the rocket and waited but all went quiet again, except for the continuing shouting from Thames Street. He took a drink of beer and called over Isaac. 'I can still smell singed hair. What is my face like?' Isaac peered at him in the gloomy light and shook his head. 'You looks like you've been six months on deck in the Indies, Master. And your hair is all burned off. You're quite a fright!'

'Look lively everyone. Something's up. Tom, are you ready?' shouted Ralph. He picked up the ramp and sighted the next rocket again. 'Ready and waiting'.

'Wait for my command'. He smiled. It was like being on ship again with his father as skipper.

'Keep your current aim. Straight at the ginnel entrance….and fire!

He lit the fuse and turned his head away, praying this rocket would work. There was the usual whoosh as it took off and he looked back in time to see it fly straight as an arrow into the ginnel entrance. There was a cry as two men jumped out of the ginnel to escape the smoke and sparks and then ran back in again.

'Yes!' Tom shouted and returned to the basket containing the remaining rockets. He lifted the cloth. Only two left. The situation was on a knife-edge. He sensed the raiders were frightened by the attack and losing their appetite for the fight. He picked up the fifth rocket and placed it in the ramp. He sighted it towards the ginnel, and stopped.

A large man was standing in its entrance, gripping a firebrand in one hand. In the other he held the collar of one of the raiders and was shaking him like a dog with a rabbit. Had someone broken through in Thames Street to come to their rescue? Maybe Jonah had a change of heart? But as he watched how the gang reacted to the stranger, an uneasy feeling grew in his chest. Even from the warehouse he could sense the anger and menace. This figure berating and cuffing the cowering members of the gang was their nemesis, not their saviour.

Tom was so sure he immediately checked the ramp was aimed at the man, and without waiting for the order, fired the fifth. The sound and light made the man turn and look. But he stood his ground, raising his left arm to shield his face, as the rocket struck home. In the light from the man's torch, Tom saw it bounce off his arm and fall to the floor. He dusted a few sparks and embers off his coat and shouted to the others. He picked up the remains and waved them in their faces.

Tom remembered Elizabeth's words. The rockets were meant to 'discourage not disable'. Their deception had been discovered. He watched in a weary daze as another figure emerged with a lit torch and, with the large man, proceeded to cajole the gang members to stay in the yard while dragging more out of the ginnel. Not for the first time, he felt the balance of the night tilt away from his family. He sensed the deflation in the room and fired the final rocket into the growing crowd assembling in the yard. Several ran off but returned seconds later. He threw the ramp into the back of the room, just missing Barty walking in from his bedroom.

He put his hand up in apology but Barty didn't notice. 'Henry is falling into a fever, Tom.' He is still awake but is soaked in sweat and agitated by the pain from his shoulder. He needs urgent medical attention.'

Chapter 32

Tallant warehouse

Tom joined his father at the window. The two men with torches had stepped forward, studying the fire closely and pointing to the warehouse roof which was now smoking.

The smaller man broke away and ran towards the ginnel, barking orders at the growing number of figures gathering there, the glow from his firebrand illuminating their faces. Tom picked up his father's eyeglass to take a closer look. The light was not good but he was sure of what he saw. 'My God. They're Apprentice Boys!' he murmured.

Over 30 figures were now in the yard, which was lit by a growing number of torches. All attempts at subterfuge had been abandoned. It was clear they were preparing a mass attack. The large man stood alone in front of the warehouse, with hands on hips, staring at the window where Tom and his father stood.

'So, you must be Ralph Tallant,; he shouted. 'And the scarecrow next to you is your son, Thomas? The man sounded surprised, then Tom remembered how he must look.

'Yes. And who are you, who has terrorised my family these past months?'

'Jack Dancer, at your service' and he made a mocking bow. 'But 'who I am' is not your concern. 'What do I want?' is the question to consider. But you know what I want, Ralph Tallant, don't you?'

Tom listened to Dancer, his language and confidence. This was no ordinary street thief. He lifted the eyeglass again to get a closer look - long greasy blonde hair, parted in the middle and hiding much of his face, but little more.

'Perhaps you can tell me,' his father replied.

'Jesu, this is tedious Tallant. I have no time to play Hood-Man Blind. And neither do you, by the look of that roof.' Tom could now see small flames breaking through several roof tiles. 'We want the map, Tallant. Hand it over and we'll disappear, and you can return to your loved ones. All your troubles will be over.'

Ralph paused, weighing up the situation. Before he could speak, Dirck pushed him aside and, running to the window, hurled a cobble at the large man. He spotted it late, jerked away, but was caught on the side of his head, making him drop to one knee. 'Thanks to you, I cannot return to my loved one, my brother,' Dirck screamed, hurling a second stone. 'My troubles will never be over and, by God, yours have only begun.' Dirck went to unleash another cobble but Petty grabbed him, pulling him back from the window.

Dancer's voice rang out again from below, now laced with cold anger. He climbed to his feet, pulling the lengthy Rondel knife from his belt. 'It's him!' Tom realised. 'The gang master who chased Robert and I to the churchyard.'

'You Dutch bastard. I'll enjoy ending you the same as your brother, on the end of a blade. Tallant, I've had enough of this pissing around. I tried to sneak in to your miserable warehouse and, until now, I was willing to let you come quietly. But too many of my men are lying hurt and now your roof's on fire, so I'm coming in, whether you like it or not.' And before Ralph could answer, he spun on his heel and walked back to the crowd of Apprentice Boys, which was still growing. As he entered their ranks, Dancer shouted a command and instantly scores of them charged forward as one toward the warehouse, screaming like maniacs.

Dirck, Petty and Sam bombarded them with cobbles but there

were too many targets. A stone whistled through the window into the warehouse and crashed against a wooden post. Soon more followed. Against such large numbers, the cobbles were not only ineffective but also providing ammunition for their attackers.

Sam fell to the floor clutching his face . Ralph ordered Dirck and Petty to stop while Tom rolled Sam on to his back. He was covered in blood and his nose badly broken. There was a shout from downstairs. Mark was keeping guard behind the front door. 'The barricade's breaking up outside! They're pulling it from the door.'

Another shout. An unmistakable shape was emerging from the ginnel. 'They're bringing up the ram. Barty, take care of Henry and Sam, and tell Andrew to keep lookout at the back. Everyone else down to the front door!'

They clattered downstairs to see Mark pushing at the barrels, chairs and tables blocking the warehouse entrance, making the barricade as tight as possible. They could hear voices outside, yelling orders. He surveyed the room and eyed up the oak wooden counter, in its position for as long as he could remember.

'Father – is this fixed to the floor?'

'No need, it's too heavy. You'll never move it.'

Petty read his thoughts and ran to the counter, shouting to Mark and Dirck to join him. Tom and Ralph followed. Together they placed their shoulders below the lip of the counter top and heaved. At first, nothing happened, but then a floor-seal of grease and dust from previous decades cracked open and the counter slid six inches across the warehouse floor.

The shouting got louder outside as Tom yelled 'if we can keep it moving it will be easier. We can do this! 'and, as he settled down to push, Sam ran to his side, linen plugs in his nose to stop the bleeding. And there was Barty on the other side. He smiled and nodded to them both, hope rising in his heart. If they could get the counter in place, blocking the door, they could hold out for longer.

'Right everyone, let's have…'

'Master Tom! Master Tom!' Andrew was running down the stairs. His spirits sagged. Had the gang evaded Jonah and were launching yet another attack from the wharf?

'What is it?

'Smoke, Master. Smoke everywhere. The pepper store is filling with it!'

'Can you see or hear any fire?'

'Not yet, Master but there's so much noise from the front of the warehouse, it's hard to hear anything!' Tom glanced at his father who appeared close to the end of his tether.

'All right. We need your eyes on our back , so return to the store and stay there as long as you can but let…'

There was an almighty crash at the front door, sending a billow of dust rising in the air, followed by a cheer from the outside.

'It's the ram. We must move this counter now. Andrew, get back upstairs!' The men got behind it again but their unity of purpose had broken, their concentration fragmented by the imminent breakthrough by the gang. The counter didn't move. The ram landed again on the door. This time the barrels were pushed back, their edges scraping along the floor. They still had over three feet to push the worktop but it might as well be three miles. When the ram cannoned into the door for a third time, there was a splintering sound and, as one, the men deserted the counter to stand ready to repel anyone who broke through.

They stood in a curve around the barricade and he surveyed their faces. He saw fear but also grim determination. 'Barty. Go back, check Henry and see whether Andrew is safe. Get him out of the store when the smoke gets too thick. Let me know if you see flames.'

His friend was close to tears. Tom reached over and squeezed his shoulder, speaking quietly into his ear. 'I know you would stay and fight, but every man must serve to his best abilities and I need you to look after Henry and Andrew.' Barty nodded slowly and then walked quickly up the stairs to the pepper store.

Another splintering crash signaled the door had finally succumbed to the incessant battering. An arm carrying a cudgel appeared through the hole, and was immediately attacked by Mark wielding a broken chair leg.

There was a pause and more shouted orders outside. 'Stand back! Stand back!'

Everyone inside took a deep breath. 'I suspect the next one will do it Tom,' so, let's see what they're made of,' Petty shouted. He thought back to his encounter with the gang leader and recalled Elizabeth's warning: 'It's a map…not worth dying for'. Would they be given a choice?

Petty's prediction was correct. In the next charge, the battering ram smashed through the door, pushed the tables and chairs back and was left stranded inside the warehouse, lying among the debris. A wave of fifteen or more Apprentice Boys scrambled over their friends, holding the ram, and jumped off the mountain of broken furniture, on to the warehouse floor.

For seconds they looked dazed but then gathered in numbers to confront the defenders. Dirck lunged at the Boys nearest to him. They instinctively backed off but then surged again as Dirck retreated. The Dutchman stood his ground and a lad at the front was pushed by the impetus of his friends into Dirck, who felled him with a chopping blow to the side of his face.

There was a howl of anger from the mob who surged again. Mark tripped and stumbled backwards. Three men grabbed his legs immediately and started dragging him back, kicking and punching at his writhing body. Tom and Dirck leapt forward, and while Isaac distracted the Apprentice Boys jabbing with his fearsome halberd, they managed to drag him away. Mark stood up, battered and dazed, but ready to renew the fight.

'Stop this! Stop, NOW!' Jack Dancer had entered through the ruined door and was standing on top of the abandoned ram. He slowly climbed down and pushed through the ranks of Apprentice Boys to confront Ralph and Tom.

'This can only end one way, Tallant. You know that. You might break a few heads, and end the lives of some of these brave boys,' and he pointed at the crowd of apprentices. 'But in the end you will be overwhelmed by our numbers, and then what will happen? I'm not sure I could control my young lads if they picked up the scent of blood...the blood of their friends.'

Andrew suddenly appeared on the stairs with Barty who was shaking his head at Tom, surrounded by a haze of smoke. The fire was spreading.

'Ah, reinforcements! Is this all you have?' Dancer laughed. 'Oh, maybe your friend has more sense than you. He doesn't seem inclined to join your fight! You know what I want, Tallant. It's simple. Give me the map and I let you all go.'

Tom desperately tried to think what to do, then Robert Petty stepped past him.

'I believe we have unfinished business first to complete. How is your arm by the way. I trust it still causes you endless pain.'

Dancer recognised Robert Petty instantly. 'You! I swore if I ever met you again, I'd tear you limb from limb, for this!' and he held up the palm of his right hand towards Robert. A livid red wound ran across the inside of his wrist. It had not yet healed.

Tom put a restraining hand on Petty's arm. 'Robert, what are you doing, goading him like this?'

Petty regarded him with his unwavering eyes. 'This man has absolutely no intention of letting anyone escape. Now, the gang have breached our defences, there will only be one outcome. We have a single chance remaining, for me to beat him, humiliate him in front of his men. That might send them off with their tail between their legs.'

'But Robert, he's a trained killer. Look at that knife'

Petty gave him half a smile. 'I know, but unlike him, I will not make the mistake of underestimating my enemy. I think I have a few advantages. I will focus on his injury and keep moving. At least it will buy us time. If that fire takes hold, he may have to abandon the building before he has found anything.' And at that, Petty turned away before Tom could protest further.

'So, let's clear the ground, and have this out, here and now', he shouted at Jack Dancer, who laughed and started pushing the Apprentice Boys back to the wrecked entrance of the warehouse.

'Actually, I don't think this would be right,' Petty continued. 'It would not be a fair fight.'

Dancer smiled. 'You should have thought about that before setting me alight.'

'No, I mean your injury disables you. It gives me an unfair advantage.'

Dancer cursed Petty again. Tom could see his friend's tactics. Infuriating the man might make his attacks more impulsive and less penetrating. 'I have only one condition.' Petty continued, his voice remaining calm. 'If I win, you and your gang leave immediately without the map. And if I lose, you may get the map but you will leave everyone unmolested. No further violence, now or ever again. '

'I have already said that.'

'Yes, but I do not trust any oath you give to us, your enemies. I want you to swear this to your men. Now.'

Jack Dancer look puzzled but shrugged his shoulders, faced the gang and made his promise. Tom could see his discomfort and realised he would be unlikely to break the oath.

'I also note you are armed. As you can see, I carry nothing. You will accept a bare hands fight?'

'Oh yes, that suits me nicely,' and Dancer drove his Rondel knife into the counter top.

Petty rolled up his sleeves. He took a swig of beer from a mug on the counter, then offered it to his opponent. This riled Dancer even more, shouting his refusal. Finally, the two faced each other, circling slowly. The crowd moved back, those who minutes earlier had cursed and threatened each other now standing side by side in rapt attention. Petty was on his toes, shifting his balance from foot to foot. The gang leader belied his name by moving more deliberately, rolling his shoulders. Tom could smell the smoke now noticeably drifting down the stair well.

Dancer lunged at Petty who swung back easily from the waist and evaded his grasp. As he swayed back, Petty punched the inside of Dancer's damaged right wrist, making him wince and shake his head. They circled again and this time Petty aimed a kick at Dancer's left knee but missed. Tom gasped as the man grabbed at his retreating foot but could not hold on. If Petty made a single misjudgment and the gang leader grabbed him, he would rapidly inflict terrible damage and the contest could be over in seconds.

Petty walked forward, offering himself to Dancer who swung his left fist, missed and overbalanced, falling forward. In a flash, Petty ran around his left side and punched him hard in the kidney. Dancer pulled up straight with a cry of pain, then paused, and let his guard drop.

Petty stepped back, keeping his fists up, his face expressionless.

Dancer spoke, his voice calm. 'Now we're fighting, I know you, brother. I've seen you grapple before and I said at the time, if I ever met this man again, I'd shake him by the hand. Best scrapper I've witnessed west of Poplar. You're with the Adventurers, aren't you?'

Petty didn't move. He was trained not to be distracted and was in a world of his own concentration. Dancer knew it.

'No matter, brother. I see you only have one thing on your mind – killing me. And that's how it should be. But I wanted you to know, before you leave this world, that you're something of a legend down the docks, and I'm proud to salute you.'

At this, Dancer put his fingers to his lips then held them before his face, like a blessing, before resuming his guard. Petty's expression – as calm and hard as marble – did not change.

'Dancer shouted: 'Let's finish this' and backed away three paces. He suddenly charged Petty straight on, who skipped to his left and grabbed Dancer's right wrist. He used the weight of the passing man to twist his grip with both hands, forcing a scream from his lips.

Despite the tormenting pain, the gang leader saw his chance and seized a handful of Petty's hair and pulled with all his strength. He was forced to release Dancer who brought his knee up rapidly and smashed it into Petty's face, making him stagger back, wiping the blood from his face. Out of the corner of his eye, Tom noticed his father walking upstairs, carrying a torch to make his way through the gathering smoke. 'Robert's fighting for his life and father's thinking about his pepper!' he thought, in disgust.

Dancer watched his opponent bend down and rest his hands

on his knees. He was struggling to breathe and a grin formed on Dancer's face. Petty moved his head to one side to blow blood from his nose and Dancer saw his chance. He ran at Petty who remained crouching, but then placed his left palm flat on the floor, and using his straight left arm to pivot, he launched his body into a horizontal arc, parallel with floor.

He timed it perfectly, delivering a scything kick deep into Dancer's left knee joint. Dancer screamed as his knee collapsed but, as he fell, he made a grab for Petty and hung on. He was now in a rage of pain and fighting on animal instincts. They were both on the floor scrabbling and kicking. Tom could see his friend was tiring and willed him to get off the ground.

Dancer used his brute strength to get an arm lock around Petty's neck who was soon gasping for breath. The veins on Dancer's forearm bulged as he strained to crush Petty's windpipe. Now he had the upper hand, the gang leader forgot about his agonising wrist and shattered knee. All his concentration focused on that headlock, his neck tendons bulging and the sweat rolling off his face. Petty's face went purple as the man tightened his grip, and slowly his legs stopped kicking. His resistance was fading and his grip on Dancer's forearm loosened.

'That's quite enough. Let him go.'

Jack Dancer looked up from Petty's face. 'What…what are you doing?'

Ralph Tallant had emerged from the pepper store, standing on the stairs, wreathed in smoke. In his hands, the map of China was burning bright.

'It's all over. You can go. We've lost it all.' he said in a flat, faraway voice. Dancer removed his chokehold and Petty's body slumped to the floor.

'How much pepper do we have upstairs at the moment, Tom?'

He looked at his father, confused. 'I could not tell you, having more important things on my mind,' looking at the lifeless form of Robert Petty on the warehouse floor.

'Oh you should always know what's in your stock. Remember what I have told you. You never know what might be there.'

Was Ralph trying to give him a coded message? His father must be finally cracking under the strain, but then he realised. The precious map had been hidden in the pepper store, where the fire was now raging. No wonder he was in shock. After all he had endured, he was to lose it after all.

'Anyway, 'tis of no matter, it will all be ash soon. As will this…' and he looked at the map, its dry paper now enveloped in flames.

'No!' Dancer was struggling to get to his feet He could not put any weight on his injured knee but held on to the side of the counter to pull himself up. 'What are you doing?' he screamed.

It had taken only seconds for the chart to be consumed with fire. It was now beyond any rescue, and Ralph changed his grip to hold it by one of its mahogany handles.

The chart had become a flaming torch which he pointed at Jack Dancer.

'It may have been the source of our wealth but it's become the cause of our misery. Perhaps it's for the best, but it is a thing of such beauty…' and, in the light of the flames, Tom could see tears coursing down his father's face.

'No. That's my money. Gone!' Dancer screamed. He pulled himself along the counter and, trailing his broken knee, lunged forward to grab Ralph.

Tom was about to fling himself onto Dancer's back and haul him down, when the gang leader stopped stock still, in front of Tom's father, and his head dropped. He crashed to the floor, revealing Dirck standing over him, the long Rondel knife in his hand, covered in Dancer's blood.

Tom saw the knife was missing from the counter and turned to his father who had dropped the remains of the blazing map. The gang leader was lying on his back, a lake of blood pooling beneath him. He bent down and examined Robert Petty. There was no sign of life. He shuffled over to the gang leader who was breathing raggedly with a deep wound in his chest.

Dancer lifted his head, trying to speak. Tom bent to listen.

'Sweet Jesus…to be done over by a sneaky Dutch shit.' The man's laugh turned into a coughing fit. 'Always thought that map was cursed. Been nothing but trouble'

'Who was going to pay you? Your brother George Tansy?'

'Oh you know about him, do you? He doesn't like you at all…I agreed when he said you had a Dutch mother.'

Jack Dancer was starting to fade. His eyes became glazed and his strength ebbed as he dipped in and out of consciousness. He lifted his head again to speak, his voice now barely a whisper. Tom put his ear next to Dancer's mouth and remained until he could no longer feel his breathing. He then sat up, transfixed by the grin on the dead man's face.

'You've killed him, you poncy bastard. You've killed Jack.' Billy Boy was beside himself with grief. 'He was my father. He was our father. He put clothes on our back and food in our bellies. Now you see what happens when you take no shit, when you won't cow-tow to the merchants and their like. When you're Jack Dancer. They kill you with your own knife when you've laid it down,' pointing at Dirck, 'not man to man. Traitorous murdering whoresons, the lot of them.'

'Do we let them get away with this? Do we?' Billy Boy screamed the question the second time and there was a roar from the crowd now packed into the warehouse. Once again Tom saw the tide of battle turning against them. But instead of an enormous weariness, a boiling rage was building inside him. He saw the weary faces of his friends, and Robert Petty still motionless on the floor. They might have lost the map, and even the warehouse, and worst of all Robert, but he would fight them to his last breath.

Without warning, a group of apprentices broke ranks and charged at Mark and Dirck. The Dutchman had dropped the knife and started throwing broken furniture at the advancing mob. Mark was waving a thick piece of landing rope above his head, lashing out at the crowd.

Tom ran at Billy Boy. A large apprentice stepped into his path and he knocked him to the floor with a clubbing right fist to his chin. Billy stepped back and whipped a poignard from his belt. He slashed at Tom who ducked and weaved to keep out of Billy's reach. Someone pushed past him and thrust a long pole at the young thief. Billy howled with pain and dropped his knife, a slashing wound in his forearm.

'Thank you, Isaac', Tom shouted over his shoulder. 'I knew that halberd would save me one day.' He glanced back and saw Isaac, grim faced and tear stained, jabbing his halberd, shouting incoherently at the mob - his master losing his senses, his warehouse burning down around him, his world crumbling.

The Apprentice Boys continued to push and gradually Tom, Dirck, Mark, Isaac and Sam were forced into a corner, guarding the body of Robert Petty. Mark's eye was bruised and starting to close and Dirck was crouching low, holding his ribs.

There was a pause while both sides gathered their breath. Many were coughing from the smoke which had reached the ground floor. 'Enough!' he shouted. 'Can't you see the fire has spread? If we don't all get out now, no one will survive this day.'

Billy Boy stepped forward, his injured arm hanging by his side. 'Not bloody likely!' he screamed at the gang. 'Come on me boys, we've got them cornered now. Finish them off and you'll be the talk of every pub in London!'

There was a ragged cheer and the gang ran at them again. Tom said a prayer as three of them barreled into him at the same time. They all crashed to the floor, kicking and punching. A finger scratched at his eyes and he bit it as hard as he could. Someone was beating his thigh while a punch in his side made him fight for breath. The weight of his attackers was crushing him and his will to resist started to drain as exhaustion set in. He had reached his limit. His head was swimming, and the sound of shouting faded. He could hear Dirck's voice, screaming in Dutch, but then nothing.

*   *   *

Tom came to, he didn't know when, to find he was no longer pinned to the floor by bodies. His side throbbed with pain and his mouth tasted of blood. He was aware of movement and talking in the room, and shouting coming from a distance.

He lay still on his back, staring at the ceiling. He blinked and Elizabeth came into view, looking down at him, her cool hand gently stroking his face 'Thank God. We made it in time. You are alive!' He smiled as her salty tears started to fall, stinging his scorched face.

Chapter 33

Bolton Hall

Tom sat in silence with Elizabeth in the living room at Bolton Hall. She held his hand as he gazed into the wood fire that was roaring in the grate, crackling and popping as the dried timber caught light. Outside, the sky was grey, the snow on the ground making the familiar garden featureless in the gloom. The door opened and he stiffened as Ralph and Beatrix walked in. His father seemed to have recovered his composure since the attack.

'How are your bruises? Does your side still hurt?'

'It's starting to feel better. If not for Elizabeth, it could have been a lot worse. In fact, I doubt I would have survived.'

His mother shook her head. 'I have still not heard the full story; how did you come to be there, Elizabeth?'

'I visited Tom in the warehouse when they were preparing for the attack. I left various…provisions,' and here she glanced at him and smiled, 'but I left troubled. It seemed logical that any attackers would use the riots as cover, and I agreed with Sir Ralph's assessment that matters on the street were coming to a head. So 'what' was going to happen seemed clear. And we knew that 'why' was the map. No, the issue on my mind was 'who'?'

'I was not sure Sir George Tansy had the resources, the manpower, to launch the kind of attack you were expecting, so I thought again about Pym. Maybe I had been wrong? I did a favour for Lucy Carlisle recently, so now I sought one in return. Would she ask John Pym if he planned to attack the Tallant warehouse?

The following day Lucy told me Pym had no idea what she was talking about. An attack on private property, especially among the merchant community, was the last thing he wanted that night. They were planning a final push against the King and, for that, he needed all their supporters on board. Any suspicion the junto was using the street protests to cover ill-disciplined score settling would cause irreparable damage to his carefully created alliances. Indeed, not only was he against any attack, he would send a troop from the Trained Bands to stop any such thing happening in his name.

'I knew something wasn't right when I saw the Apprentice Boys in the Yard.' Tom added. 'Pym had expressly stated they should stand down on the night to ensure the protest was orderly.'

Elizabeth nodded. 'Guarded by two of our servants, I came into London. The City was in turmoil but Pym's people and the militia walked us through the barricades and blockades to Thames Street, which was a complete press of people. I was aghast when we arrived and saw your roof burning. But within minutes men from the Trained Bands had flooded the warehouse, ordering the Apprentice Boys to stand down. Without their support, the gang fled into the night. I will always remember that scene: Tom down, and poor Robert Petty…everyone else hurt and exhausted. I knew we had arrived with only minutes to spare. I was…'

There was a commotion in the next room, and raised voices. The noise increased and Peter strode into the living room, a flustered servant in tow.

'The King has fled! He has left London.' Peter shouted, waving his arms in the air. 'Ran away to Hampton Court with his tail between his legs. We have won! We have won! I don't believe it!' Tom had never seen his brother so excited.

'Peter! Are you sure?' Beatrix asked as she stood and hugged her eldest son.

'Well, *I* can well believe it,' Ralph growled. 'He's abandoned his palace, Westminster and the Tower! Given them to Pym and his cronies. What idiocy! It makes you want to weep. He's the King, for Lord's sake!' he snorted. 'Peter. How are you? We're talking about the terrible events in the city two days ago.'

Peter pulled up a chair and joined them by the fire. 'How am I? Exulting in the Lord's victory! And this is only the start! It's hard to take in, that this moment has finally arrived,' And Peter's flushed, beaming face stared at each of them in turn.

'Terrible events? Oh, you mean the street protests?' Peter continued breathlessly.' It is regrettable people have been hurt but the riots were inevitable, I'm afraid, after the King trampled on the privileges of Parliament by marching into the Chamber. Tom, I hear we have you to thank for John Pym's escape with the others?'

Tom waved his hand dismissively. 'I asked Peter to come because I thought he might be able to shed light on who attacked our warehouse the other night.'

'Yes, I did hear something about an attack.' Peter said, calming down. 'I was coming here to find out if the rumours were true when I heard the wonderful news about the King.'

'The warehouse is badly damaged,' Tom replied. 'Thank goodness there was more snow later in the night or we'd have lost the roof. As it is, our entire pepper stock is ruined.'

'That's dreadful! Was anyone hurt? How did it happen?'

'How did it happen? – that's the question. We know a mob of Apprentice Boys were involved, so we thought you might have some idea, given your contacts. You've used them before to keep the pot boiling when pushing for Puritan reform.'

Peter looked puzzled. 'Strange that I have not heard about it.'

'Very strange, considering you arranged it.'

Silence again. This time shocked.

'What on earth do you mean?' Peter shouted.

'Oh, come Tom…' his father added.

'Do you think a dying man would lie?'

'Brother, you are talking in riddles. Are you drunk?'

'What has a dying man got to lose? He may as well speak the truth. I mean Jack Dancer. That name must be familiar to you Peter. No? Jack Dancer, the gang leader who you were paying to steal the map?

'Dancer lead the attack on the warehouse. He was mortally wounded by Dirck and, as he lay dying, I asked if George Tansy was his paymaster. Robert Petty had a theory that Tansy was behind the whole thing. Dancer confirmed Tansy was his brother but, by now, he was fading fast and it was difficult to understand all he said. His final utterance was a single word: 'Judas'. But as he expired, his face broke into a dreadful smile.

'From Dancer's few words, I got the impression he and his brother shared a hatred of the Dutch and had reached some form of agreement to attack us. So when he said Judas I assumed George had somehow betrayed him in the end.

'But I had no evidence of that, and I couldn't rid myself of that single haunting image – Dancer's death mask, a mocking grin. I was beginning to wonder if he was telling me something else, perhaps that the betrayal was mine, not his. And then I heard Elizabeth's news.'

'What news? Oh Tom, what are you saying?' his mother cried. 'Peter wouldn't be involved with those dreadful people who tried to kidnap to kidnap Ellen., and killed poor Jan. Your brother couldn't be responsible for his death.'

'Peter was seething. 'You base this accusation of me, your own brother, on a villain's smile, as he died! What if this criminal was trying to place a doubt in your mind? Has it not occurred to you that an animal like him was intent on one final destructive act, to mislead you and turn you against your own brother – and you fell into his trap? I am mortified you could think me capable of such villainy.'

'You said the gang leader was a criminal.' Elizabeth's steady voice cut through the emotion. 'You said …an animal like him. Do you know him?'.

'No, of course not.'

'So why describe him as an animal?'

'Well he must have been, to lead such an attack. This is desperate stuff. Why have you both taken against me so?'

'Because I saw you.' Elizabeth again. Calm. Inexorable. 'That was the news I gave to Tom.'

'Saw me where? Who are you to be involved in my family affairs? What business is it of yours? It seems to me you are trying to insinuate yourself with my parents to gain their favour.'

'Peter!' Beatrix exclaimed. 'If you spent more time with your family you would know that Elizabeth has become a firm friend to me, to us. If not for her, we could easily have lost Tom last year, when he almost drowned in the Thames.'

'It is alright, Beatrix. Peter is right not to believe me with such a serious accusation. We do not know each other well. But Simon Atkins, would you believe him?

'What? Well, yes, of course. Simon is an esteemed brother in the movement. But what has he got to do with this web of lies you are weaving?'

'On John Pym's orders, Simon Atkins led the troop that broke up the attack on your family warehouse. I know because I was with him, and we both saw you there, on the fringes. Go and ask him, Peter. Simon will confirm it.

'Oh, this is absurd. You said the attack happened at night. It was dark!'

'The people near you were holding firebrands. We saw you Peter. So how had you only heard rumours of what happened if you were there? Because you are lying to your family. Believe me, knowing how much this is hurting your mother, I would not say so if I was not absolutely sure.'

Beatrix searched Peter's face. 'Peter? Look at me! I need to know the truth. I demand the truth!'

Her eldest son stood and paced the room, stopping at the window. Outside, the clouds were heavy again with the threat of snow and one of the first flakes had stuck to a window pane. Peter placed one finger on the inside of the window, over the snowflake. He paused, thinking, then lifted his finger. The snowflake had disappeared. He turned and faced the room.

'There is a mighty war coming. Any day now. Between the godly and our Papist loving King. Anyone who does not believe that is deluding themselves. 'The country will split into two. We have God on our side but we are under no illusions that the King has a large number of misguided followers. So the numbers in both camps could be close.

'Whosoever can find a singular advantage could gain control. Otherwise we must anticipate a long, bloody campaign, brother against brother, father against son' and here he looked at Ralph and Tom. 'It could take years. However, it could be different. I can lay my hands on such a singular advantage and end the struggle swiftly. I just need enough money.'

'Do you mean more soldiers? Mercenaries? I wouldn't put my trust in them,' Ralph said. 'Also I'm not sure either side will appreciate foreigners involved in a family quarrel.'

'No, not mercenaries. Instead a battalion of honest godly Englishmen, committed to the cause.'

'But everyone will have chosen which standard to fight under,' Tom replied. 'Where will you find additional recruits in

England in sufficient numbers? '

'I won't need to. They are waiting for me now, in America.'

Silence again.

'We have planned this for the last six months. We have over 2,000 patriots, trained and ready to return, to be armed and fight for the cause, with more to come. We will charter a fleet to bring them back, once we have the money. Yes, the journey will take months, but this conflict will not be finished overnight.'

'My God,' Ralph whispered. 'It could be done and they would make a difference. But how would you make it happen?'

'I overheard a conversation between you and Uncle Jonas four or five years ago about a map you had acquired in the east. I was intrigued, so I did more eaves-dropping and discovered it was the source of much of our trading intelligence, ancient knowledge of the China seas that kept us ahead of our rivals, allowing us to navigate safely around reefs and other dangers to reach new trading centres which our rivals did not even know existed.

'When I became desperate for a large sum, I remembered the map. If I took the chart, I could offer it to other merchants and name my price. I searched the house and the warehouse without success. Time was running out. With war becoming inevitable, I needed the money now. So I sought professional help. I spoke to various people. The same name kept cropping up: Jack Dancer, ruthless and determined, but also intelligent and resourceful, blessed with an education. I offered him a large fee to find the map on the condition that no one in the family would to be hurt. That's why he planned the first raid on Bolton Hall when you were out.'

Tom held his hand up and Peter paused. 'So you're telling me that, the very morning we met in the Bull Inn at Old Palace Yard and you promised to protect the family, at that precise moment you knew this gang was rampaging through our home?'

'I'm sorry. That was one of the reasons I agreed to meet you then, to get you out of the house. As I said, I didn't want any Tallant near Jack Dancer's men when they got to work.'

'Peter, whatever happens in the future, I'm afraid I can never trust you again, brother. Never.'

'Well I regret that greatly. It is a burden I will have to bear, one of the many I have undertaken in the name of the Lord's work.'

Tom said nothing; just glared at Peter, shaking his head.

'You didn't want the family to be hurt, but what about the deaths of two Jesuit priests?' Elizabeth said. 'Presumably, they did not matter because they were Catholics.'

Peter turned on her. 'What is this now? Another attempt to blacken my name. I have no idea what you are talking about!'

'What is this, Elizabeth?' Beatrix asked.

Tom interrupted. 'Robert Petty had been investigating the murders of two Jesuit priests before the break-ins started. But what have these got to do with Peter?'

'Ever since your father showed us the map, I have wondered how a European merchant - English, Dutch, Spanish, whoever - how could they use the chart, as all the descriptions are in Chinese - the name of towns, natural features, the navigational instructions. They would need someone who understood Chinese but could also speak the European language they used.

Where would you find such a person? I thought about sailors and asked Isaac if he'd ever met a Chinese mariner in London, who'd maybe washed up in the city and never gone home. He said there had been one, many years ago, but the only English he knew was on-deck instructions and an impressive list of curses.

'I had reached a dead-end but my mind wouldn't let the matter drop. Then I realised the Jesuit murders had stopped when the break-ins started, which seemed more than a coincidence. Tom, you'd said the Jesuits had been executed expertly by a professional killer, and when I was told about Dancer's brutal fight with Robert at the warehouse and heard about his reputation, I was convinced he was responsible for the death of the priests.

'But why would he do that? Then it came to me last night in a conversation with my parents. My father was reading out a pamphlet, another warning about papist plots, telling Catholics to keep out of our country and go back to where they belonged, with the savages, working as missionaries . Missionaries...and it was there, staring me in the face.'

'Elizabeth, I'm sorry but what are you talking about?' Ralph interjected. 'I think we are getting off the point...'

'The villain! What a serpent...' It was Peter, slamming his fist on the table.

"Yes, Peter. You said Dancer was intelligent, and he was too clever for you. When you described the map to him, he saw at once it would be more valuable and easier to sell if he could also provide a person who could translate all the precious navigational information which was written in Chinese.'

'Jesuit missionaries!' Tom cried out. 'Barty told me they travelled all over the world spreading the faith. As far as North America...and China.'

'My guess is Dancer was looking for a Jesuit priest who could speak and write enough Chinese to translate the map. I can only assume the first two he found suffered the misfortune of undertaking their missionary service elsewhere and, for that, they forfeited their lives. Once they knew Dancer, he couldn't afford to let them live.'

'So he murdered two priests because of information I gave him?' Peter said.

'Yes. I also don't think he had any intention of handing the map over, once he'd secured it. He was intelligent enough to know its value, particularly if he also had someone to translate it.'

Peter held his head in his hands. Tom had never seen him so reduced, his usual confidence and energy had disappeared.

'I knew nothing about this. I intended to let the buyer find a translator. I didn't have time to look myself. After the first raid, Dancer took it upon himself to try another tactic to force father to cooperate - the kidnap attempt on Ellen. I was furious and said if he tried anything like that again I would cut our deal and tell the authorities. He didn't like that and threatened me but I pointed out that I had my own army, so he agreed to continue. That would be when he stopped looking for Jesuits. He realised he needed to find the chart as soon as possible, and make a quick sale, before I had a change of heart and turned him in.

'On the night of the final assault I repeated my order not to harm you, hence the sneak attacks,' Peter continued. 'But when I saw the fire spreading and your resistance holding, thanks to those damned rocket devices, I decided we were running out of time and needed to swamp you with bodies, so I called in the Boys. Then Dancer lost his senses when he saw Robert Petty and everything went wrong.

'So now you have neither map nor money,' Tom added.

'Thanks to you, father. When the map was on fire, why didn't extinguish the flames?'

'As the fire in the warehouse spread, I ran up to the pepper store which by then was well alight. The pepper sacks were burning and I could hardly breathe. I battled my way to the chart's hiding place only to find the map was already in flames. It all happened so quickly, there was nothing I could do. It's a grievous loss to the company.'

The room fell silent, as all present absorbed the revelations.

Finally, Sir Ralph spoke again: 'Peter, I find it hard to believe what I have just heard. You were prepared to steal from your own family, something you knew could bring financial ruin…'

'Pah to financial ruin!' Beatrix interrupted. 'It's cost the lives of two good men and left others injured.'

'But I told Dancer not to harm you…'

'So the lives of others do not matter?' His mother was shouting now, red in the face. 'And scaring your sister so much she has bad dreams and no longer wants to leave her room?'

'My purpose was higher,' Peter bridled. 'I was doing God's will. Raising an army to defend the godly and spread the truth.'

'The truth!' Beatrix exclaimed. 'Do not insult my intelligence Peter by claiming to be an upholder of truth!'

Peter's voice became detached and cold. 'Don't worry mother. I can see how you feel. As soon as my affairs are in order, I will leave England.'

'Oh Peter, no,' his mother gasped. 'So this is my punishment for trying to save my son, showing him the error of his ways. This is too cruel.'

Peter softened. 'It is not a punishment, mother. In truth, there are bigger matters at stake than the future of one family, even my own. There is much to do in America, recruiting and training more men to hopefully join the fight here in England. We will have to find other vessels, perhaps one or two at a time, but every shipload will help.

'One thing I know, in my heart and soul, is that war is now with us, and it will be a long and bloody affair. But with the Lord's will, the godly will triumph, and the King brought under our yoke.'

Chapter 34

On the River Thames
January 11th, 1642

Jonah Dibdin powered his wherry across the Thames with a serene smile on his face, at his feet a small basket containing a bottle of East Indian Arrack, with seal intact.

He caught Tom's eye and nodded. He had never seen Jonah so content. 'That's taken very kindly, thank you,' he said, effortlessly maintaining a rapid stroke. 'I will share it with the boys who helped.' Tom doubted this but, not wishing to spoil Dibdin's rare good humour, did not voice his reservations.

'It is a gift from the Tallant family, for your help defending our warehouse.'

'As I said, I was defending the river and, for that, I receive it gladly.' Elizabeth was smiling, nodding her head. 'Well said, Jonah.'

He studied the weathered face of the boatman. Was that a faint blush appearing? He refused to believe it. Not Jonah.

Today the boatman was making a rare excursion west of London Bridge, visiting his elderly mother near Temple Bar. To do this he had passed under London Bridge at the exact time the swell was level. It suited Tom because he wanted to travel to Westminster.

A cold breeze gusted up the river and Elizabeth moved closer to him, linking arms. Jonah was now focused on the regular rhythm of his rowing, looking over their heads at the bubbling wake of his wherry. With each stroke the towering presence of St. Paul's came closer on their right.

'I know the weather is wintry Tom, but I needed a private

place to talk. This will not be an easy conversation but you should know all that I have discovered.'

Tom was about to speak, but thought better of it.

'The story of the map is a complicated one, and I need to complete it for you. You've just learned how your father acquired the chart and attempted to keep its existence secret. But there is one remaining chapter to this story.

'Do you remember, when we first met, you told me that you fell into debt trading on the tulip market in Amsterdam?' Tom nodded but said nothing. It was five years ago, but he was still paying the price of his disastrous tulip speculation and it remained a sensitive subject. He wasn't sure he was ready for this at the moment.

'Do you also remember telling me that your Uncle Jonas paid your debt at the time and then it was transferred to your father's account. It was an enormous figure and you never knew how Ralph managed to secure the loan.

Tom looked up with a start. 'You're not saying it was…

'Yes. He offered the map to the bank and, ever since, that chart has been acting as security for your family's loan while it's gradually being paid off. Your mother told me…yes, this is something Ralph *has* shared with Beatrix, because he needed her signature on various documents at the time. She's never mentioned it to you because she didn't want to add to the guilt you felt about your tulip misadventure.

'So why was the map not stored in an Amsterdam bank vault? The lenders would have to sell it if your father ever defaulted on the debt payments, and so they required possession. Apparently, your father argued that the map was required to plan future trading expeditions, to make money to pay off the debt. The bank reluctantly agreed to this, but only if he insured it against loss. Luckily Amsterdam has some of the largest merchant insurance companies in the world and he was able to arrange cover. It increased the cost of the loan but he had no choice.

'When the attacks started at Bolton Hall, Ralph guessed someone was after the map. If he lost it, his debt was covered by the insurance but the all the invaluable trading knowledge on the chart would transfer into a rival's hands. Plus there was still much for Ralph to learn from the Chinese inscriptions. So keeping the map at that stage was imperative to him.

'But I noticed he quickly changed tack following your mother's row with him, and I was puzzled. He agreed quite readily to her demand that the map be removed, and then installed it in your warehouse, right in the centre of the City. It was more vulnerable there, but he didn't seem to care. He could sense the warehouse would be attacked but instead of moving the map to another safe place, he built up the defences and said, in effect, come and try and get it.

'Why would he do this? And then I remembered a conversation I had with him a week earlier. I was bringing him up to date on my research into longitude and I mentioned the documents about Joan Bleau that Beatrix had translated for me. Your father seemed very interested but didn't mention them again. Days later Beatrix told me that he had asked to see the papers himself and had studied them for hours.'

'But that's good, isn't it? He was showing an interest in your work?'

'Yes, but it seemed an all consuming interest, even at a time when he was trying to deal with the attacks. For Ralph to take this information so seriously, I knew it must be linked, but I could not deduce how. So I studied the information again, and I saw it.'

'Saw what?'

'Exactly what your father had realised. Joan Bleau was

producing a new portolan chart of the China Seas that was so detailed it would begin to open up that area for European merchants. Within a few years, the value of your father's Chinese map would tumble. Its exclusive hold on this knowledge would crumble.

'And when the map lost its value, the banks would require additional security on the loan?'

'Exactly. So, suddenly, everything changed for Ralph. Now the map had to be destroyed, and quickly, while he could still claim the full insurance value and pay off his debt. But he also needed to satisfy the insurers that it was not destroyed deliberately by his hand, but as the result of a robbery or an accident.'

'Well, at least that did happen. Father did not set fire to the warehouse. He cannot be blamed for that.'

Elizabeth paused. 'After you had been rescued from the warehouse, I went back to look in the pepper store. It was full of smoke but, I have to tell you Tom, the fire had not spread there, despite what your father said. It was still confined to the roof timbers. I could see a pile of pepper sacks that had been pulled away and next to them I found the map's storage box .'

'Which was not charred?'

She shook her head.

'So, he must have set fire to the map.'

'Yes. He used the torch he was carrying which he then threw out of the loading hatch. I discovered it smouldering on the wharf below when I left the building. It was imperative to your father that the map wasn't stolen. It would still be valuable for a number of years and give his rivals a big advantage for a time. No, it had to be destroyed, and in a way that appeared he could do nothing to save it.'

'So all his talk of 'financial ruin' is not true?'

'The company will lose money on the pepper spoilt by smoke

damage, but the big threat – not being able to support your loan – will be averted by the insurance pay out, which will take place thanks to your father's trickery.'

'But what about poor Robert and Jan; all the injuries, the harm and damage, to create this deception?'

She said nothing. Simply gazed into his eyes.

'I said recently that I was worried about your father's behaviour, and I'm afraid I am not surprised by my discovery. He has only one thing on his mind – the continued growth of your merchant business. That directs all his thoughts and actions. It must be very worrying for your mother.'

'But this is all my fault! If I hadn't lost all that money during the tulip mania, my father would not have had to take out the loan.'

'That is true Tom. But you were younger and made an innocent, no a foolish, mistake. But you were never told what actions would then be taken to put it right. Your father could have sold the map to cover the debt. He had already extracted some valuable trading information from it, thanks to Jonas. But he didn't want anyone else to get it. I sense, for him, it's all about being cock of the walk. There's plenty of spice trading to go round but he doesn't like to share, and that includes problems and decisions with your mother.'

Tom reflected on what Elizabeth said and shrugged. He could not take all of this in. He needed more time. Then another thought occurred to him.

'Do you think he knew Peter was behind the attempts to steal the map, that somehow they colluded?'

'No. It would not make any sense. He didn't want anyone to get the map, including Peter, who would only have sold it on to a rival merchant.'

Tom thought more about Elizabeth's explanation and gave a hollow laugh. 'So, in the end, all this has been a family dispute, my father against my brother!'

'They're cut from the same cloth, both driven, and in my opinion, ruthless if needs be. You take after your mother, thank God.'

'That sounds like England,' Tom added. 'Our family has experienced what awaits us all. Father against son. Husband against wife. Brother against brother. It will be a horrible.'

'With too many victims, and not only on the battlefield.'

'Like mother?'

'Yes. You must stay close to Beatrix. You can see how she is hurting. She must feel very uncertain at the moment and will need you more than ever in the months ahead.'

She squeezed Tom's hand and they fell silent, listening to Jonah's regular breathing and the creak of his oars as they were pulled through the water.

'I keep thinking about Robert, how he stepped in to save us all by challenging Dancer.'

'That was Robert. That was how he lived and how he met his death. He saw what was going to happen and calculated he had a chance of defeating Dancer.'

'But if we had known Pym was going to step in and save us, he still could have been alive today.

She turned to him. 'I have thought of little else in recent days, if I could have got there sooner, but I believe it still would have been too late. Without Robert's intervention, Dancer would have overwhelmed you all much earlier. Then his promises to Peter about saving the family would have been worthless. It wasn't just me who saved you. It was the time Robert bought for you by challenging Dancer and taking him on.'

Tom's memory returned again to the fight in the warehouse but he pushed it away. 'Yes, we all have reason to thank Robert and will keep him in our hearts, as we must Barty who is devastated.'

Elizabeth moved back, her eyes troubled. 'And this is not the only grief to afflict me. Today I received a letter from a fellow astronomer. Galileo is no more. He has died in Italy, still under house arrest.'

'I'm so sorry. I know he was your hero. He first inspired your interest in science. I thought you....you would be ...'

'Distraught? Yes, so did I. I think Robert's death has given me a new perspective. Perhaps I am growing up. Also, Robert has gone and I will remember him fondly but it is final. But I feel Galileo lives on through the knowledge he has left behind, to be studied further and better understood. That really matters.

'It's something I have learned from Lucy. Life is fleeting and I need to achieve as much as I can with all the knowledge I can acquire. Like Robert's death, I mourn Galileo's passing but I can also honour his existence by achieving as much as possible with the gifts he has left. We must learn all we can, in the uncertain times we face.'

There was a cheer ahead. Dibdin glanced over his shoulder to see a small fleet of craft travelling up the Thames, their pennants bobbling and snapping in the brisk wind. In their centre was a larger rowing boat.

'Jonah, can you get us a little closer?'

The waterman effortlessly increased his stroke rate, surging forward to draw level with the other wherry. Tom could now see five men sitting in the middle and immediately recognised John Pym and Denzil Hollies.

He pointed to the boat. 'It's the five MPs – now the King's gone, they must be returning to the Commons! They will get a great reception.' Elizabeth nodded, staring at the scene with her eyes shaded from the bright winter sun.

Jonah effortlessly kept pace with the small fleet of craft. Everywhere, Tom could see smiling, excited faces, full of hope.

Then his mind returned to the King, isolated but defiant, brooding in the cold and empty Palace of Hampton Court, and he feared for the future.

Endnote

London, December 1641, was famously described by Royalist Sir Robert Slingsby as 'the maddest Christmas that I ever saw'.

To the contemporary witness that might have been an understatement as both law and order and respectful political discourse finally collapsed – leaving fertile ground for this author to interweave fact with fiction.

In 'The Wrecking Storm', the major historical events and some of the people are real, but not their interaction with my characters. The dramas in the Commons witnessed by Thomas did take place. Lucy Carlisle did exist and her changing loyalties have been well documented. The Selden Map, remarkably like the one destroyed in the Tallant warehouse, is currently housed in Oxford's Bodleian Library. With a little imagination, could we see it as the twin to the chart owned by Ralph Tallant?

For more about the history, I would recommend:
The Leveller Revolution by John Rees
Mr Selden's Map of China by Timothy Brook
Court Lady and Country Wife by Lita-Rose Betcherman

For more about the Tallant family, 'Rags of Time', is the prequel to 'The Wrecking Storm' which introduces us to Thomas, Elizabeth and one of the most interesting periods in English history.

As ever, it's great to hear from readers of my books. You can contact me via mike@mikewardmedia.com .

Michael Ward

Printed in Great Britain
by Amazon

24865496R00128